EXPLORE AMST

2024

Your Complete Pocket Guide with Insider Tips for an Unforgettable Trip, Canal Cruises, Perfect Itinerary, and More on a Budget

Ethan Foster

Copyright © 2024 by Ethan Foster

All rights reserved.

No part of this publication may be reproduced, distributed, or transmitted in any form or by any means, including photocopying, recording, or other electronic or mechanical methods, without the prior written permission of the publisher, except in the case of brief quotations embodied in critical reviews and certain other noncommercial uses permitted by copyright law.

Disclaimer for Images: Photographs and illustrations in this book have been sourced from personal experience, various individuals, and organizations. Neither the publisher nor the author shall be liable for any loss of profit or other commercial damages, including but not limited to special, incidental, consequential, or other damages.

Table of Contents

MAP 8

UNTAPED AMSTERDAM BEAUTIFUL IMAGES 10

WELCOME TO AMSTERDAM 16

RECENT FACTS ABOUT AMSTERDAM 20

ABOUT AMSTERDAM 26

    BRIEF HISTORY AND CULTURE 28

        Culture of Amsterdam 29

    WHY VISIT AMSTERDAM IN 2024 32

        Visiting Amsterdam as A Wheelchair User or Someone with Limited Mobility 39

        Challenges in Accessibility 39

        Getting Around Amsterdam with Mobility Issues 40

PLANNING YOUR TRIP 42

    BEST TIME TO VISIT 43

        The Best Time to Visit Amsterdam 43

        Cheapest Time to Visit Amsterdam 44

        Least Busy Time to Visit Amsterdam 45

        Worst Time to Visit Amsterdam 46

        Amsterdam in Spring 47

    Amsterdam in Summer 48

    Amsterdam in Autumn 49

    Amsterdam in winter 50

   BUDGETING AND CURRENCY TIPS 52

    Currency in Amsterdam 52

    Amsterdam Travel Costs 52

    Backpacking Amsterdam Budgets 54

    Money Saving Tips 55

   VISA REQUIREMENTS (LATEST 2024 UPDATE) 58

   TRANSPORTATION GUIDE 62

   ACCOMMODATION OPTIONS 64

MUST-VISIT ATTRACTIONS 82

   SEE ANNE FRANK HOUSE 83

   VISIT THE VAN GOGH MUSEUM 84

   VISIT THE RIJKSMUSEUM 85

   EXPLORE JORDAAN 86

   RELAX IN VONDELPARK 87

   TRY THE HEINEKEN EXPERIENCE 88

   OUR LORD IN THE ATTIC MUSEUM ONS' LIEVE HEER OP SOLDER 89

   CENTRAAL STATION 91

   RED LIGHT DISTRICT 92

Verzetmuseum Amsterdam	94
Body Worlds	96
ARTIS Amsterdam Royal Zoo	97
Museum Het Rembrandthuis	98
Concertgebouw	100
A'dam Lookout	102
Dam Square	103
Moco Museum, Amsterdam	104
The Amsterdam Dungeon	105
Het Scheepvaartmuseum	The National Maritime Museum	107
Royal Palace Amsterdam	108

EXPERIENCING AMSTERDAM CULTURE 110

Best Places to Eat in Amsterdam	111
Dutch Cuisine and Culinary Delights	126
Coffee Shops vs. Cafés: A Local Experience	134
Nightlife and Entertainment	140
Month by Month Festivals and Events	148
Shopping in Amsterdam	156
Luxury Shopping Streets in Amsterdam	*157*
Fashion	*160*
Jewellery	*161*

Beauty 161

Furniture and Lifestyle 162

Food 162

Tax-free shopping 163

CULTURAL ETIQUETTE AND LOCAL CUSTOMS 164

The Function of the Family 164

Dutch manners 164

Egalitarianism 164

Dutch Privacy 165

Meeting and greeting 165

Gift-Giving Etiquette 166

Dinner Etiquette 166

Building Relationships and Communication 167

OUTDOOR ACTIVITIES AND DAY TRIPS 170

HAND-PICKED CYCLING ROUTES 171

Why Rent a Bike? 171

City Centre Route 172

Amsterdam Woodland Route 174

WATER ACTIVITIES 176

WINDMILLS AND TULIP FIELDS 180

Windmills in Amsterdam 181

Windmills on Just Outside of Amsterdam 184

Best Tulip Fields in the Netherlands 185

How to Get to Tulip Fields 189

Dutch Tulip Fields Season 189

Tulip Field Tips 190

ICE SKATING 192

SPORTING EVENTS AND VENUES 194

PRACTICAL TIPS AND RESOURCES 196

SAFETY AND HEALTH INFORMATION 196

ESSENTIAL DUTCH PHRASES 198

PHOTOGRAPHY TIPS 200

USEFUL APPS AND WEBSITES 202

THE BEST BOOKING RESOURCES 206

CONCLUSION 208

ITINERARY 209

3 DAY ITINERARY 209

7 DAY ITINERARY 212

14 DAY ITINERARY 215

FREQUENTLY ASKED QUESTIONS 219

ABOUT THE AUTHOR 224

Amsterdam is known as the "Venice of the North" because of its huge canal system. Amsterdam's canal network is three times longer than Venice's, with more than 100 kilometers (60 miles) of canals and 1,500 bridges.

Amsterdam staat bekend als het "Venetië van het Noorden" vanwege zijn uitgebreide grachtenstelsel. Met meer dan 100-kilometer aan grachten en 1.500 bruggen is het grachtennetwerk van Amsterdam drie keer zo lang als dat van Venetië.

Ámsterdam es conocida como la "Venecia del Norte" debido a su extenso sistema de canales. Con más de 100 kilómetros (60 millas) de canales y 1,500 puentes, el sistema de canales de Ámsterdam es tres veces más extenso que el de Venecia.

Explore AMSTERDAM | 8

Map

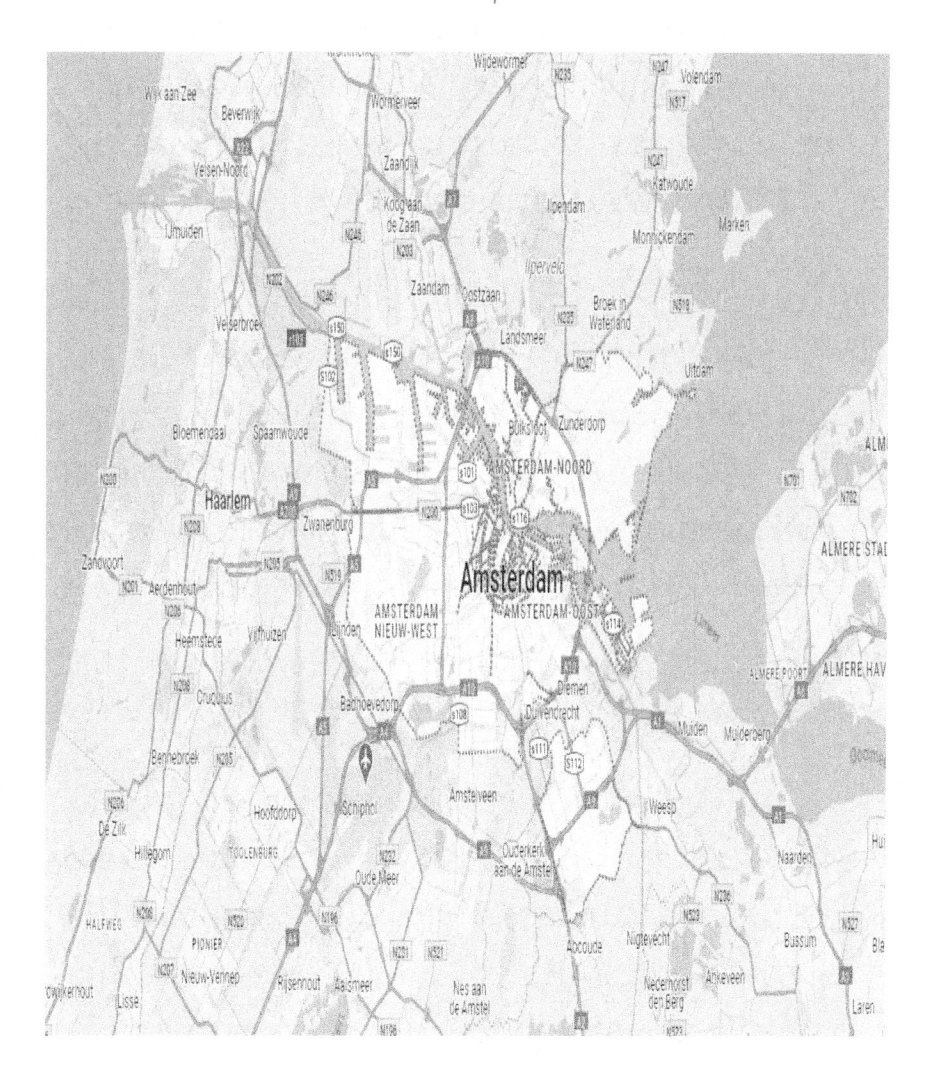

Amsterdam is widely regarded as the "Bike Capital of the World." With about 881,000 bicycles in the city and more bikes than residents, it's no surprise that cycling is one of the greatest ways to discover Amsterdam.

Amsterdam staat bekend als de "Fiets Hoofdstad van de Wereld." Met ongeveer 881.000 fietsen in de stad en meer fietsen dan inwoners, is het geen verrassing dat fietsen een van de beste manieren is om Amsterdam te verkennen.

Ámsterdam es conocida como la "Capital Mundial de la Bicicleta". Con aproximadamente 881,000 bicicletas en la ciudad y más bicicletas que habitantes, no es sorprendente que andar en bicicleta sea una de las mejores maneras de explorar Ámsterdam.

Explore AMSTERDAM | **10**

Untaped Amsterdam Beautiful Images

Explore AMSTERDAM | 11

Explore AMSTERDAM | **12**

Explore AMSTERDAM | 13

Explore AMSTERDAM | 14

Explore AMSTERDAM | **15**

Welcome to Amsterdam

Greetings, brave travelers, and welcome to an adventure unlike any other! Buckle up as we reveal Amsterdam's secrets, not in the pages of conventional guidebooks or on the great expanses of the internet, but directly in your hands. This is more than simply a guidebook; it's your ticket to an Amsterdam journey beyond anything you've ever imagined.

Amsterdam, known for its attractive canals, antique windmills, and tulip-drenched vistas, has more hidden treasures than one might expect. Prepare to be enchanted by the fascinating collision of old and new, where time-honored traditions merge with surging modern vitality.

This isn't your average travel companion. We've gone above and beyond to discover the city's hidden gems, curate exclusive experiences, and disclose secrets that Google would be embarrassed to divulge. It's more than simply a guidebook; it's a key to a hidden world that unlocks the actual spirit of Amsterdam.

Imagine cycling along gorgeous canals, discovering tucked-away street art, and indulging in culinary pleasures at hidden jewels known only to locals. Our tour is more than just locations; it is about creating an experience personalized to your preferences.

Have you ever longed to tour a floating flower market at sunrise, or learn about the history of a quirky neighborhood's street art? Our insider insights ensure you don't miss a beat, giving you an advantage over the average tourist.

Discover Amsterdam beyond the postcard. We've delved into the city's pulsating pulse, conducting interviews with inhabitants who reveal their favorite haunts, secret customs, and the greatest places to see a spectacular sunset.

Have no fear! Our meticulously created itineraries appeal to everyone's preferences, from cultural aficionados to night owls seeking the city's explosive pulse. Maximize your stay with easy, stress-free arrangements.

But wait—there's more! We have teamed up with Amsterdam's top venues to provide exceptional benefits. With this guidance, you will not only explore but also indulge. Unlock hidden menu items, gain preferential access to must-see activities, and receive discounts at handpicked eateries.

Forget standing in line - our guide provides direct contacts to avoid lines at renowned museums, allowing you to spend your valuable time exploring rather than waiting.

Fancy a private canal sail beneath the stars? With our guide, you can schedule one-of-a-kind experiences that are tailored to your preferences, transforming your visit into a personalized masterpiece.

You now hold the key to an extraordinary Amsterdam adventure. This is more than simply a guidebook; it is an invitation to discover the city's secrets, create amazing experiences, and immerse yourself in an Amsterdam that few have the opportunity to experience.

Embark on a trip where each page reveals a fresh revelation and each recommendation is a hidden gem to be unearthed. Amsterdam is calling, and this guide will help you plan an adventure that will be the pinnacle of your travel experience.

Prepare for an Amsterdam experience that Google and TripAdvisor cannot deliver or rate. Let the adventure begin! Your exclusive journey into the heart of Amsterdam awaits!

Explore AMSTERDAM | 19

Recent Facts about Amsterdam

You've heard of the canals, coffee shops, tulips, and bikers in Amsterdam. You have Van Gogh's masterpieces and the Anne Frank House on your must-see list. Your restaurant reservations and tour tickets are in the bag. But what are you missing from the Netherlands' largest and most exciting city?

These fascinating facts reveal a side of the Dutch capital you may not have known, such as how it keeps above water and where its tropical citizens are located. Impress your friends and make your stay in Amsterdam even more intriguing with this acquired information.

The Metropolis Stands Atop Eleven Million Poles

Amsterdam is two meters (6.6 feet) below sea level and constructed on soft peat and clay, so staying above water requires a significant feat of engineering. To summarize the entire history, which can be seen in the

Amsterdam Museum, 11 million wooden beams prevent the city's structures from sinking. Wooden piles have been installed in Vondelpark to prevent trees from sinking into the naturally swampy ground.

You Can Cruise 100 Kilometers on The Canals

If you've ever wanted to live on a houseboat, Amsterdam is the city for you. With over 165 canals, you may travel 100 kilometers (60 miles) without leaving the city limits or crossing the same canal twice. Impressive for a city that is just roughly 15 kilometers wide. A one-hour canal trip cannot cover all of the waterways, but it is ideal for seeing the highlights, such as the quirky 17th-century buildings, lovely bridges, and great landmark museums.

Every Sip of Europe's Most Popular Beer Is Brewed Here

While most European countries have at least one major local beer brand, the Netherlands can boldly claim to have the most popular. Heineken was founded in Amsterdam in 1864 and currently produces about 200 million hectoliters (5.2 billion gallons) of golden nectar each year. And, whereas some companies work with local brewers in each area to produce their beers locally and save on shipping expenses, Heineken makes every print in-house. At the Heineken Experience, you'll learn about the brand's history and manufacturing process before enjoying a frosty glass straight from the source.

The Canals Are Busy with Bicycles and Boats

Regular visitors to Amsterdam are well aware of the city's cycle lanes. With more bikes than dwellings in the city, the canalside cycle lanes function as small highways, and it's all too easy to get in the path of traffic, especially during rush hour. Perhaps this explains why 25,000 motorcycles are fished from canals each year. Perhaps one too many Heinekens is involved? While we do not recommend taking your ride for a quick swim, a private bike tour is still the greatest way to explore the city's lesser-known areas. Your guide will be well-versed in Amsterdam traffic rules to keep you on dry land.

Anne Frank's Diary Is Available in Seventy Languages

The Anne Frank House, one of Amsterdam's most renowned attractions, offers a fascinating glimpse into the city's darkest period and its best-recognized WWII occupant. The Anne Frank Tour tells the complete narrative of the Nazi-occupied city and the secret annex where the Jewish Frank family lived in hiding for two years, from 1942 to 1944. Thirteen-year-old Anne's famous journal recounts their existence at Prinsengracht 263 and is so gripping that it has been translated into 70 languages, allowing her narrative to be relayed all over the world.

Vondelpark Is Filled with Parakeets

Northern Europe isn't the first location you'd expect to see a flock of colorful parakeets, yet you'll find them in Vondelpark and trees across the city. Around 4,000 vivid green tropical birds live in Amsterdam. But how? According to one urban legend, a truck carrying exotic birds overturned, allowing its cargo to escape and settle in the park. Others claim that a woman released a mating pair of parakeets. The only certainty is that they prosper in this odd setting - keep an eye out for them when touring Vondelpark and the city's landmarks.

The Houses Are Narrow for Good Reason

The lovely houses that flank the canals in districts like Jordaan are known for their slim silhouettes. In reality, the narrowest has a two-meter-wide facade. This unusual architectural method has a simple explanation: tax. Back in the 17th century, Amsterdam citizens were taxed based on the width of their property, therefore the narrower your home, the lower your annual tax cost.

Heineken Was Founded in Amsterdam

Heineken is currently a popular beer all over the world, although it originated in Amsterdam at The Haystack Brewery. Gerard Adriaan Heineken made the first Heineken Lager in 1873. In 2011, around 2.7 billion liters of Heineken lager were brewed. If you want to understand more about Heineken and its history, visit the Heineken Experience in Amsterdam.

There Are More Museums Per Person Than Nearly Anywhere Else

Amsterdam, although a relatively tiny capital city with a population of little over a million, stands out in terms of culture. Amsterdam has 85 world-class museums, trailing only museum-heavy towns like Paris, Vatican City, and Washington, DC in terms of museums per capita. When you've seen enough masterpieces at the Rijksmuseum, Van Gogh Museum, and Stedelijk Museum, visit the Moco Museum for modern art or the city's more unusual collections. Street art in STRAAT? Movies at the Eye Film Museum? Fresh veggies at the Cannabis Museum? It is all here.

Amsterdam Hosts the World's First Floating Flower Market

Although Amsterdam is well-known for its tulips, the Netherlands produces a wide range of other flower types. The small country accounts for more than half of the global flower trade. There is also a floating flower market, the only one of its sort. This 160-year-old market was originally established as a hub for traders who delivered their wares by barge and congregated around the canals. The market is now a more permanent fixture, a vibrant landmark that smells as lovely as it looks, and it is available to the public every day except Sunday. It's the ideal place to pick up some fresh flowers while also learning about the local culture.

Amsterdam Has More Bridges and Canals Than Venice

Amsterdam was once a modest fishing community, but its proximity to the sea made it an appealing trade destination in the 1600s. The city expanded rapidly, and the Dutch government soon began to construct bridges and canals to connect the various areas of Amsterdam. As a result, Amsterdam now has over 1,200 bridges, more than three times as many as Venice. There are approximately twice as many kilometers of canal. They're nice to walk over, but the finest view is from a canal boat. A package that includes a walking tour and a canal boat allows you to do both. Of course, you can enjoy the view and take photos along the way.

It Wasn't Always Named Amsterdam

The Dutch capital is now known as Amsterdam, although it was previously known as Amstrelredam. The name is said to date back to 1275 and refers to a dam built across the Amstel River to avoid flooding. As the city flourished, its name was condensed and streamlined, and Amsterdam became the standard.

Amsterdam Hosts the World's Oldest Stock Exchange

If money is your thing, the Amsterdam Stock Exchange, founded in 1602, is the world's oldest stock exchange and continues to operate today. A bronze bull sculpture near its entrance is a reproduction of Wall Street's famed Charging Bull statue, which stands outside the New York Stock Exchange. Following a merger with the Paris and Brussels stock exchanges, it is currently known as Euronext. Tours are available to learn more about its history and to see inside.

Amsterdam Is the Gay Capital of Europe

The Netherlands became the first nation in history to allow same-sex unions in 2001. Amsterdam is a renowned tourist destination for the LGBTQ population, and the annual Amsterdam Gay Pride event draws a large throng each year.

About Amsterdam

Welcome to Amsterdam, a city that seamlessly blends historical elegance and a modern enthusiasm for life. Amsterdam, located in the heart of the Netherlands, is a city with winding canals, tulip-lined alleys, and centuries-old buildings that provide a gorgeous backdrop for your next memorable visit.

Amsterdam, known for its relaxed attitude and friendly residents, welcomes you to explore its cobblestone streets on foot, by bicycle, or by navigating the city's famed canals. Don't be shocked if a funny canal boat comes by, carrying locals sipping coffee or tourists taking photographs with historic bridges in the background.

Amsterdam is a cultural melting pot, offering a diverse range of experiences. Visit the world-renowned Rijksmuseum to learn about Dutch art and history, or wander around the quaint Jordaan area, which is full of unique stores and cafes. For a more daring adventure, hop on a bike and explore the city like a true Amsterdammer, admiring the beauties of blossoming tulips and bright street art.

As diverse as the city's canals are, so is its gastronomic culture. Local stores sell traditional Dutch specialties, but cosmopolitan areas offer world sensations. And don't forget the legendary Dutch cheese—no trip to Amsterdam is complete without a cheesy experience.

In Amsterdam, the pleasure does not end with the sun. The city's nightlife is famed, with everything from quaint brown cafes to packed nightclubs. Whether you love live music, stand-up comedy, or just a drink by the water, Amsterdam has something for any nighttime traveler.

So pack your luggage and prepare to experience Amsterdam's diverse magic. From historic monuments to hidden jewels, this city is ready to amaze, delight, and make your vacation unforgettable. Prepare to fall in love with Northern Venice, where every street and canal has a story to tell. Amsterdam awaits, and adventure calls!

Brief History and Culture

According to history, Amsterdam was formerly a village on the Amstel River. It expanded during the Middle Ages and eventually became a significant commerce center. In 1275, the people of this area were granted the privilege to convey goods by water through Floris V's (Count of Holland) realm. The small town of Amstelledamme expanded when they obtained additional rights from the bishop of Utrecht in 1306. In 1323, this town became a port for Hamburger beer. The herring trade expanded rapidly with the introduction of herring curing in 1385, which kept fish fresher for extended periods. However, over time, this metropolis became increasingly vulnerable to fires. First in 1421, then in 1452. The second was particularly devastating, and wood was outlawed from being used as a building material.

The Schreierstorn Tower, Waag Gatehouse, and other significant structures were built in the late 14th century. The 17th century saw an

increase in Amsterdam's population and the construction of three unusual canals. Amsterdam's population increased as more immigrants arrived. There were plague outbreaks that killed a lot of people, yet the population continued to grow. The Athenaeum Illustre opened in 1632 and was renamed Amsterdam University in 1977. The Industrial Revolution contributed to the transformation and development of this metropolis. However, it also led to certain societal issues.

The Rijksmuseum, Central Station, the Stedelijk Museum, and the Rembrandt House Museum were open from 1885 until 1911. The city saw riots in 1917 as a result of food shortages during World War I. New housing developments were erected, and in 1928 the Olympics were held. Many Jews were forced to leave the city during WWII. Following these battles, Amsterdam grew swiftly. New museums, including the Van Gogh Museum, Joods Historisch, Foam Photography, and Diamond Museum, opened in the late twentieth and early twenty-first centuries.

Culture of Amsterdam

As an arts center, Amsterdam has a lot to offer. There are 40 museums, which draw approximately four million people per year. The Rijksmuseum (State Museum) is renowned for its collection of 17th-century Dutch masterpieces. The Stedelijk (Municipal) Museum houses a world-renowned collection of modern art. The Van Gogh Museum showcases the art of Vincent van Gogh and his contemporaries. Other notable museums include the Anne Frank House, the Amsterdam Historical Museum, the Dutch Maritime Museum, and the Rembrandt House.

There are almost 200 live-performance venues, including the Concertgebouw, which houses the world-famous Royal Concertgebouw

Orchestra, and the Muziektheater, where the national ballet and opera companies appear. The city also has two universities (the University of Amsterdam, founded in 1632, and the Free University, founded in 1880), as well as other academies and conservatories. Many cultural visitors visit the inner city (and parts of the suburbs) to see the excellently preserved canal-side homes of the Golden Age as well as the other historic sites, including the Royal Palace. The arts have a significant economic impact in Amsterdam, employing thousands of people and earning about $1 billion in revenue annually. There are almost a hundred galleries, including prominent auction houses.

The recreational facilities are substantial. The Amsterdam Woods, the beach town of Zandvoort to the west, Sloter Lake (Sloterplas) in the heart of the western suburbs, and many smaller lakes to the south and north of the city all provide chances for outdoor activities. This densely populated city has over 40 sporting parks, clubs for practically every sport, and more than 250 open-air tennis courts. World-class spectator sports venues include the Amsterdam Arena, which is home to the Ajax football (soccer) team, and the Olympic Stadium.

Explore AMSTERDAM | **31**

Why Visit Amsterdam in 2024

As with many prominent European towns, you may wonder if Amsterdam lives up to its reputation. You may even wonder if Amsterdam is worth visiting. As someone who has visited Amsterdam, I will answer this question and highlight some of the city's wonderful attractions.

First and foremost, I fell in love with Amsterdam, thus I believe it is worth a visit. It is a wonderful city with a variety of activities to suit everyone's interests. Here are seven of my favorite reasons to visit Amsterdam.

It's Canals

Amsterdam's renowned canals are a must-see and defining feature that distinguishes the city as a distinct and captivating destination. The scenic rivers that wind through Amsterdam provide tourists with an unforgettable experience, allowing them to immerse themselves in the city's rich history, breathtaking architecture, and dynamic culture.

These rivers, listed as a UNESCO World Heritage Site, provide a wonderful backdrop to the city's scenery, which is dotted with historic buildings, picturesque bridges, and busy streets.

Furthermore, the canals are more than just tourist attractions; they provide an authentic sense of local life. They serve as a vital focus for Amsterdam residents, with houseboats lining the water's edge and locals riding along the banks, resulting in an authentic and active atmosphere.

Whether it's capturing the perfect photograph of the iconic canal houses or simply enjoying the serene beauty while savoring a stroopwafel from a nearby vendor, Amsterdam's canals weave an enchanting tapestry that truly captures the city's charm, making it a must-see for any traveler.

I enjoyed my wheelchair-accessible canal boat excursion. During my brief visit to Amsterdam, I had the opportunity to view several of the city's main attractions. It was also an excellent method for me to gain my bearings and make mental notes of places I wanted to return to once I was on land.

Accessibility to Amsterdam's canals: Canals can be explored on foot or by boat. As previously indicated, there is also a wheelchair-accessible canal boat excursion available. This tour is accessed by a motorized lift from the boat's floor. Once onboard, you can opt to either inside at an accessible table or outside with unimpeded views. Amsterdam is a cultural metropolis and a must-see trip for art fans, including some of Europe's top art museums. The city's art scene is magnificent, with world-renowned institutions housing a staggering collection of cultural artifacts. At the forefront lies the Rijksmuseum, a crown gem known for its enormous collection of Dutch Golden Age classics like Rembrandt's "The Night Watch" and Vermeer's "The Milkmaid."The Van Gogh Museum, which houses the world's largest collection of Vincent van Gogh's paintings, sketches, and letters, rounds off this formidable roster. It takes guests on an intimate trip through the legendary artist's head and spirit, allowing them to delve deeply into his creative progress and emotional depth.

Each museum adds something distinct to the city's cultural tapestry, making Amsterdam a refuge for visitors looking to immerse themselves in the colorful and diverse world of art.

Accessibility in Art Museums: All of Amsterdam's most popular art museums accommodate wheelchair users and provide extra assistance for individuals with impairments. Step-free pathways are available, as are mobility aids such as manual wheelchairs, as well as specialist excursions for those with impaired vision and cognitive issues like dementia. Make sure to check the museum's website for availability and other information.

Visiting the Anne Frank House

Visiting the Anne Frank House in Amsterdam is a deeply moving and historically significant experience that enriches any visitor's visit to the city. The house where Anne Frank and her family hid from the Nazis during World War II offers an insight into the life of a young girl living through the horrors of the Holocaust. Stepping into the covert annex where Anne wrote her famous diary brings history to life, eliciting emotions and instilling a deep sense of empathy and introspection.

The Anne Frank House tells a captivating story, leading guests through hidden rooms, showcasing personal objects, and sharing Anne's passionate remarks. It serves as a poignant reminder of war's tragedies as well as the human spirit's endurance.

Furthermore, the museum encourages reflection, and stimulating talks about tolerance, human rights, and the need to oppose discrimination. Accessibility of the Anne Frank House

The museum hosting Anne's original journal is handicap accessible. The attic where she and her family hid is not accessible (there are steep and narrow steps). However, the museum does provide an unusual virtual reality tour of the attic for persons with mobility issues who are unable to visit it firsthand.

Tulip Season is Gorgeous

Tulip season in Amsterdam is a beautiful display that captivates visitors from all over the world, making it an unbeatable reason to visit this bustling city. Typically peaking from late March to mid-May, the city transforms into a riot of color as millions of tulips blossom.

The sheer beauty and range of tulip kinds on exhibit are amazing, with rows upon rows of expertly manicured tulip fields painting the countryside in vibrant shades of reds, yellows, pinks, and purple. Keukenhof Gardens, also known as the "Garden of Europe," is a must-see trip during this season, with a stunning display of tulips as well as other bulb flowers such as daffodils and hyacinths. Visitors can stroll through carefully constructed gardens, snap breathtaking images, and learn about the history and development of tulips from many exhibits and displays.

Beyond Keukenhof, the countryside around Amsterdam transforms into a tapestry of beautiful blossoms, and many people take scenic drives or bicycle trips to see these picturesque fields.

Whether you're a horticulture enthusiast or simply looking for natural beauty, the tulip season in Amsterdam provides an unparalleled visual feast, leaving visitors astounded by the sheer magnificence of these iconic flowers and providing an unforgettable experience that captures the essence of Dutch springtime.

Accessibility to Tulip Season in Amsterdam: Tulips are commonly seen across the city and in public gardens during the spring season. There are some accessible trips to the Keukenhof Gardens and the countryside available; however, always check with the tour company to see if they can suit your requirements.

For example, some can store your mobility gadget, but you must be able to ascend the bus's stairs. Others may have lift-equipped vehicles, allowing you to remain in your wheelchair.

Popular Day Trips from Amsterdam

Haarlem: One popular day trip option is to visit the historic city of Haarlem, which is only a 15-minute train journey from Amsterdam. Haarlem's cobblestone streets, beautiful architecture, and prominent sites like the Grote Kerk (Great Church) and Frans Hals Museum provide a fascinating cultural experience.

Utrecht: Furthermore, a short train ride to Utrecht reveals a dynamic city decorated with canals, medieval structures, and the famous Dom Tower. Utrecht combines historical charm with modern flair, making it ideal for visiting its vibrant cafes, one-of-a-kind boutiques, and scenic waterways.

Zaanse Schans: For those seeking natural beauty, a trip to the windmill-dotted countryside of Zaanse Schans is essential. Zaanse Schans, just a short bus ride away, provides an insight into the traditional Dutch way of life with well-preserved ancient windmills, wooden cottages, and artisanal craft exhibitions.

Amsterdam Is a Cyclist's Paradise

If you enjoy cycling, Amsterdam should be high on your bucket list. Bicycles are the major form of mobility in the city, and they are easily rented by visitors.

In reality, Amsterdam is known as one of the world's most bike-friendly cities, with a vast network of well-maintained cycling pathways that make it extremely convenient and safe to go by bike. For bikers, experiencing Amsterdam offers a unique opportunity to immerse themselves in the Dutch lifestyle while taking in the city's iconic buildings, beautiful districts, and picturesque canals at a leisurely pace.

Furthermore, there are several possibilities to go out of the city and see the beautiful countryside, either on your own or on a bike tour.

Amsterdam Is Worth Visiting Because Of Its Nightlife

The city is well-known for its diverse and welcoming party scene, which includes everything from bustling taverns and quaint pubs to trendy nightclubs and live music venues. The dynamic energy pulsing through Amsterdam's streets after dark produces an exciting atmosphere that attracts both locals and tourists.

Furthermore, the city's calm and open atmosphere fosters a vibrant and inclusive nightlife scene. Visitors can enjoy a drink at one of the many traditional brown cafes or a fashionable rooftop bar with breathtaking city skyline views.

Whether you're searching for a lively club scene or a more relaxed evening by the canals, Amsterdam's nightlife has a distinct appeal that guarantees an amazing experience for anyone looking to immerse themselves in the city's after-dark offers.

While the famed Red Light District is the obvious pick for nightlife, other neighborhoods like Leidseplein and Rembrandtplein are also excellent possibilities.

Accessibility in the Red Light District: Most of the area's narrow streets and alleyways are cobblestoned, making it difficult to navigate in a wheelchair. However, recent years have seen initiatives to improve accessibility.

Some businesses, such as cafes, restaurants, and specific shops, have made concessions with ramps or accessible entrances, however, this is not consistent throughout the district. Furthermore, certain adult entertainment establishments may be wheelchair accessible, while others may not be due to the historic character of the structures.

Before visiting Amsterdam's Red Light District, it is recommended that tourists with accessibility needs plan ahead of time, research specific sites, and inquire directly with venues or companies about accessibility amenities.

Visiting Amsterdam as A Wheelchair User or Someone with Limited Mobility

As a wheelchair user, I thoroughly enjoyed my time in Amsterdam. While no place is completely accessible to everyone, I found that the city provided a variety of enjoyable experiences that allowed me to immerse myself in its culture.

In the preceding part, I attempted to include as much information about accessibility as possible so that you could get a sense of the amazing Amsterdam tourist sites that are accessible with a disability. However, I will also discuss some of the potential obstacles and impediments to accessibility so that you know what to expect during your visit.

Challenges in Accessibility

During my time in the city, I encountered two significant barriers to accessibility. The first one was cobblestones. Cobblestones were common in Amsterdam, as they are in most older European cities.

The second problem was that bikes, vehicles, and other objects frequently blocked the sidewalks, making it impossible to navigate. There were moments when I had to use the bike lanes that run alongside many of the sidewalks (which is not ideal because riders can easily run over you).

I expected both of these to be an issue during my journey and made the best of it, often looking ahead to see which way would be the best/safest for me to take. Another reason I appreciated the canal boat tour was that it allowed me to view so much of Amsterdam without having to worry about these barriers.

Getting Around Amsterdam with Mobility Issues

In general, Amsterdam is a walkable (or rollable) city with many popular attractions in a relatively small area. The sidewalks will be busy and cobblestoned, but they will also have curb cuts.

If you want to save electricity (and battery power), you can make use of the city's tram system. The latest trams will be the most accessible, featuring a wheelchair symbol near the accessible door (which is level). In addition, there will be a designated wheelchair spot on board.

Explore AMSTERDAM | **41**

Planning Your Trip

Traveling to Amsterdam is more than simply a holiday; it's an exciting adventure through a city where every corner tells a tale. To ensure that your visit is nothing short of spectacular, meticulous planning is your guide. This chapter delves into the complexities of organizing your trip to Amsterdam, including insider tips, practical advice, and handpicked recommendations that go above and beyond the norm. Whether you're a first-time traveler or a seasoned explorer, let's plan a journey that's just right for you. From selecting the best time to come to navigating the city's picturesque maze of canals, this chapter will guide you through a flawless and amazing Amsterdam trip. So, tighten your seatbelts and prepare to delve into the finer elements that will transform your Amsterdam trip into a planning masterpiece.

Best Time to Visit

I am looking for the ideal time to visit Amsterdam. Then you are in luck! As a frequent traveler to the Dutch capital, I've seen the city in spring, summer, and fall. If that wasn't enough, I'll be taking my first winter vacation to Amsterdam in just a few weeks!

Over the years, I've grown to adore this renowned European getaway. I first visited the capital for my twenty-first birthday and did not return until a year ago. Since then, it has been my second home, and I will be returning for the sixth time in December.

If you're a first-time tourist, you might be wondering when to go. Should you visit the capital during tulip season or outside of peak times? When it comes to touring Amsterdam, each month has its own set of advantages and disadvantages, and it might be difficult to pinpoint a certain season.

In this guide, I will explain all you need to know to make an informed selection. By the end of this tour, you'll know when and why you should visit this lively city. Let's get to it!

The Best Time to Visit Amsterdam

The greatest time to visit Amsterdam is from June to August. The weather in Amsterdam is ideal during these months, with temperatures ranging from 50°F to 70°F.

Additionally, outdoor activities and festivals are in full flow. Having a drink on the canal terraces is essential, and riding is the most pleasurable. Everything is in blossom, ready for guests to take advantage of the longest days of the year in mid-summer.

Popular events during this period include:

- The Holland Festival (June-July) is the country's oldest and largest performing arts festival, comprising theatre, music, opera, modern dance, visual arts, and film.
- Amsterdam offers a variety of events, including Taste of Amsterdam (June), Awakenings Festival (July), Amsterdam Gay Pride (August), and Grachtenfestival (August), all focused on music.

Finally, if you plan to visit Amsterdam during this period, we recommend booking your stay in advance because it is the busiest season. Also, read our guide to the ideal times to visit Europe (the shoulder seasons)!

Cheapest Time to Visit Amsterdam

If you're on a tight budget but still want to visit Amsterdam, consider visiting between November and mid-December, or mid-January and February.

It is thought to be the most affordable time to visit Amsterdam because of the cheaper accommodations and aircraft tickets available.

Unfortunately, the cheapest time to visit Amsterdam corresponds with the "seemingly" worst time to be there (at least in terms of weather).

For further information, specifics, and popular activities during this period, please see our section on the worst time to visit Amsterdam below.

Least Busy Time to Visit Amsterdam

Amsterdam is usually crowded, but the least crowded times to come are in the spring (April- May) and fall (September–November).

These two seasons are ideal for visitors who want to take advantage of shorter lines in front of galleries and museums, easily secure restaurant reservations, and, overall, enjoy a slightly less crowded Amsterdam.

Spring and October are both beautiful times to see the colors and changes in nature in this city. For example, in the spring, tourists can appreciate the splendor of the city's freshly blooming tulips, while those visiting in the fall will enjoy the shifting colors.

For the former, visit Amsterdam in the last two weeks of April and the first two weeks of May, and don't miss out on seeing the Keukenhof Flower Garden; for the latter, keep in mind that the first week of November is the best time to view the leaves.

If you visit Amsterdam in spring, expect average lows of 39°F and highs of 61°F. If you travel in the fall, expect average temperatures ranging from 39°F to 64°F.

Popular events in the spring include:

- Celebrate National Restaurant Week (April) with a variety of great dining selections.
- King's Day (April) with orange-themed events.
- The Tulip Festival (April) celebrates the new spring season.
- Independence Day (May) commemorates the country's independence during World War II.

If you visit Amsterdam in the fall, consider the following events:

- UNESCO World Heritage Weekend (September): a collaboration between the country's ten World Heritage sites.
- Amsterdam Fringe Festival (September): an artistic mix of theatre, dance, and performance.
- TCS Amsterdam Marathon (October): a World Athletics Platinum Label Road Race with options for full, half, or 8K.
- Amsterdam Light Festival (November-January): a true light extravaganza.

Worst Time to Visit Amsterdam

Winter (December—March) is the worst time to visit Amsterdam. It's cold, with temperatures ranging from 39°F to 44°F, the sky is gloomy, and the atmosphere can be depressing at times.

Outdoor activities are mainly off the table. But it's the greatest time to go ice skating and visit museums.

However, winters in Amsterdam may be beautiful if you visit for the festivities, such as the Christmas markets or the New Year's extravaganza.

If the Christmas markets pique your interest, here are the ones worth seeing in and around Amsterdam: Amsterdam Winter Paradise, Funky Xmas Market, Pure Markt Wintermarkt, The Sustainable Christmas Market, and Edam's Lichtjesavond.

Whether you're shopping for last-minute Christmas gifts or just want to enjoy the festive atmosphere, these Christmas markets have you covered.

Other interesting events include:

- Valhalla Festival (December), a cirque animale incorporating electronic music such as deep dance and techno mix, coupled with acrobatics, clowning, freak, and peep displays.
- New Year's Dive (January) is a yearly Dutch tradition of leaping into the North Sea on January 1st; are you brave enough to join the Dutch?
- New Year's Dance (January) is a party ritual that continues New Year's celebrations.
- Tulpendag (January) celebrates the tulip season with thousands of displays along the Dam.
- Amsterdam International Fashion Week (January) attracts fashion enthusiasts.

Amsterdam in Spring

We've already covered why spring is the greatest season to visit Amsterdam, but what if you're not a fan of tulips? Fortunately, there are numerous reasons to visit the city between March and May.

It's a great time of year to go outside because the weather is pleasant but not too hot. From boat excursions and botanical gardens to informative walking tours, you may spend days discovering the city's sights and sounds.

Are you looking for something more thrilling? Then head to the A'DAM Lookout. After taking in panoramic views of the city, confront your worries by swinging over the edge of Europe's largest swing. As frightening as it sounds, it's one of the most unusual things to do on your Amsterdam vacation!

As if that weren't enough, this popular European country hosts a plethora of fascinating events, including Open Tower Day and Kings Day.

Amsterdam in Summer

If you want to experience the greatest weather, visit Amsterdam during the summer. However, given the uncertain weather in England, I cannot offer any assurances...

While my weekend journey in June was bright and sunny, my two-week trip in August was cloudy and rainy. Finally, when visiting the Netherlands, make sure to pack for all weather conditions.

Rain or shine, there are numerous reasons to visit the city during this time of year. Not only is the capital at its liveliest, but it's also the best time of year to see the famed canals. You can tackle the water on your own or take a guided tour with one of the many boat companies available.

If the weather is nice, you should seriously consider taking an open boat excursion. These allow you to catch some sunlight and see the city from a different angle.

After taking canal excursions on all six of my travels to Amsterdam, it's one of my favorite ways to spend time. Especially while holding a glass of wine or a bottle of Heineken (wink wink).

In terms of events, the city hosts numerous music festivals and events throughout the summer. Perhaps the largest and most thrilling is Amsterdam Pride.

Thousands of travelers from around the world gather to celebrate love and the LGBQT2+ community. After personally experiencing Amsterdam during Pride, I can say that it's one of the best occasions to visit the Dutch capital.

The Netherlands was the first country to legalize same-sex marriage, therefore the city has a unique aura. Visiting the city during this time of year is like attending a gigantic party!

Amsterdam in Autumn

Are you planning a cozy getaway? Then Amsterdam is an excellent choice for an autumn city holiday. As the temperature cools and fewer tourists visit the city, you may see a more relaxed side to the Dutch capital.

If you want to avoid rain, September is often the best month to visit the city outside of high season, so keep that in mind.

In Amsterdam, October often brings dreary skies with the occasional sunny day.

As autumn draws to a close in November, fewer visitors visit the Dutch capital. As one of the quietest periods to visit this popular destination, it's worth thinking about experiencing the city without crowds of other people.

On the occasional sunny day, autumn is a wonderful season to take day travels to local sites. For example, you may take a train to Haarlem, Zaanse Schans, or Zaandam to see a different aspect of the Netherlands than the capital city.

There are numerous events throughout the autumn season, just as throughout the year. Some of the most renowned include the Amsterdam Dance Event, Museum Night, and the Amsterdam Light Festival.

Amsterdam in winter

If you don't mind rain and uncertain weather, visiting Amsterdam in the winter is an excellent way to save money. Accommodation is more economical this time of year, making it less expensive to explore the city. Outside of the holiday season, you'll see fewer tourists, making for a more peaceful experience.

Christmas celebrations generally begin in November, when Sinterklaas comes to the Dutch capital. By mid-December, the city has Christmas-themed markets, ice rinks, and winter wonderlands brimming with festive cheer. Haarlem is a great destination to celebrate this exciting time of year!

Are you thinking about going on a winter adventure outside of Christmas? Don't worry! This is one of the greatest seasons to visit Amsterdam's major museums since you can avoid the frigid temps in favor of world-class exhibits. Traditional Dutch cuisine is another excellent way to warm yourself after a day of exploration. While it's (obviously) tasty year-round, it's especially good in the winter.

I can't suggest The Pantry enough. This is unquestionably one of the top restaurants in Amsterdam, serving a variety of delicious Dutch meals. When I noticed a line on my way to a cocktail bar (which is typical for me), I decided to stop and check what the buzz was about. Wow, I'm glad I did.

This quaint establishment delivers some of the city's most wonderful meals. From calming stamppot to sweet tiny pancakes, it's a must-see for local food.

Moeders, a popular restaurant across town, delivers equally delicious food. Make sure to visit at least one of these establishments during your stay in the Dutch capital. You will not regret it, believe me!

Explore AMSTERDAM | **51**

Budgeting and Currency Tips

Currency in Amsterdam

The Euro is the official currency of the Netherlands, issued and supervised by the De Nederlandsche Bank. If you buy travel money online, you may see the official code - EUR. Euro prices are likely to be shown in businesses and restaurants with the currency sign €.

Once you arrive in the Netherlands, you will find the prices of items displayed in EUR, and you will need to start paying for things in local coins and notes, which are commonly found in the following denominations:

Banknotes: 5, 10, 20, 50, 100, 200, 500 EUR; coins: 1, 2, 5, 10, 20, 50 cents; 1. 2 EUR.

Amsterdam Travel Costs

Hostel costs - If you choose a centrally located hostel, expect to pay between 18 and 30 EUR per night for a bed in a dorm of eight or more beds. A 4-6-bed dorm costs around 30-50 EUR per night. Prices remain generally stable throughout the year. A private twin room with an en suite bathroom costs 85-115 EUR per night. Free Wi-Fi is standard, however, just a few hostels offer self-catering amenities. Only a few provide free breakfast.

Budget hotel rates - Budget two-star hotels start at 80 EUR per night (most average around 125 EUR), however, there are a few new pod hotels in Amsterdam that provide a single pod for around 60 EUR. Basic amenities include free Wi-Fi, a television, and a coffee/tea maker.

Airbnb is available throughout the city, however it has grown increasingly controlled in recent years. A solitary room starts at 80 EUR per night, while an entire apartment costs roughly 175 EUR per night (but you can find units for less than 150 EUR per night if you book early).

Food - Dutch cuisine consists primarily of veggies, bread, and cheeses. While meat has not been as prevalent historically, it is now a dinnertime staple. Breakfast and lunch are typically open-faced sandwiches with cheese and cold cuts. Dinner is a "meat and potatoes" meal, with meat stews and smoked sausage being popular options. For those with a sweet tooth, the stroopwafel (a waffle cookie with syrup filling) is the go-to pick, while apple tarts/pies are also popular locally.

The famous FEBO serves cheap meals (such as burgers and fries) for roughly 5-6 EUR, but don't expect anything special. Other street foods, such as pizza pieces, shawarma, and falafel, cost between 3 and 8 euros.

There are numerous low-cost fast-food restaurants in Amsterdam, including McDonald's, Maoz, Wok, and Walk (the finest by far). Combo lunches (like McDonald's) here cost between 9 and 10 EUR. Many eateries in the city offer prix-fixe lunch deals priced between 10-15 EUR.

Mid-range restaurant dinners begin at roughly 35-40 EUR for a three-course meal with a drink. Vegetarian and pasta dishes start at 12 EUR, and a beer costs around 5 EUR.

In a high-end restaurant, a five- or seven-course menu costs between 80 and 100 EUR, with a glass of wine costing roughly 6 EUR.

A cappuccino or latte costs between 3.50 and 4 EUR, while a bottle of water costs roughly 2 EUR.

Cafe de Jaren, Pancakes, Modoers, Café Papeneiland, and Burger Bar are among my favorite restaurants.

If you prepare your meals, plan to spend between 50 and 60 EUR per week on groceries such as pasta, veggies, poultry, and other staples.

Backpacking Amsterdam Budgets

If you're backpacking in Amsterdam, expect to spend around 60 EUR each day. This budget includes living in a hostel dorm, taking public transportation, cooking the majority of your meals, minimizing your alcohol consumption, and participating in free activities such as walking tours and lazing in parks. If you intend to drink, allocate at least 5-10 EUR each day to your budget.

A mid-range budget of approximately 165 EUR covers sleeping in a budget hotel or private Airbnb, dining out at cheap local eateries, enjoying a few drinks, taking the occasional cab to travel around, and participating in more paid activities such as visiting museums or taking a cuisine or art tour.

On a "luxury" budget of 280 EUR or more per day, you can stay in a hotel, eat out whenever you want, drink as much as you want, take more taxis, rent a bike or car to explore outside of the city and participate in whatever excursions and activities you desire. However, this is only the ground floor of luxury. The sky's the limit!

You can use the chart below to get an estimate of how much you should budget daily based on your travel style. Keep in mind that these are daily averages; you may spend more or less on certain days. We merely want to provide you with a rough notion of how to create a budget. Prices are in Euros.

	Accommodation	Food	Transportation	Attractions	Average Daily Cost
Backpacker	25	15	10	10	60
Mid-Range	75	45	20	25	165
Luxury	100	105	35	40	280

Money Saving Tips

Amsterdam is one of Europe's most popular tourist destinations—and one of the most expensive. Every year, costs rise, especially since COVID. Fortunately, a stay here does not have to break the bank, as there are several methods to save money in Amsterdam:

Get the I Amsterdam Pass - which includes free admission to most major museums and sites as well as free public transportation. If you plan on visiting several museums, purchase this card. The pass starts at 65 EUR per day.

Drink at hostels - Hostels offer the finest drink discounts in cities. Even if you don't stay there, most have public bars with 2 EUR beers and other drink promotions. Belushi's Bar at The Winston is also quite popular with the locals.

Get the Museumkaart (Museum Card) - This card is valid for a year and allows you to visit museums in Amsterdam and beyond for only 64.90 EUR. The Museum Card provides entrance to dozens of institutions in Amsterdam and hundreds around the Netherlands. It is available for purchase in select museums and is an excellent choice if you intend to spend a significant amount of time in the Netherlands.

Take a free walking tour - For an overview of the city, join one of the free walking tours. New Europe Tours offers the largest one, which will provide you with a thorough introduction and overview. Just make sure you tip!

Grab an Amsterdam Nightlife Ticket - This ticket is valid for two or seven days and costs 10-20 EUR. It provides you with unrestricted entrance to eight clubs, a welcome drink at five of them, access to the Holland Casino, savings on Uber rides, and more. If you plan on partying in Amsterdam, this nightlife ticket will undoubtedly save you money.

Hire your boat - Rather than taking a costly canal trip, charter your boat. If you have three or four individuals, it costs roughly 20 EUR per person and allows you to bring wine, food, or smoke on it. Boaty Rentals (also known as Amsterdam Rent A Boat) provides excellent possibilities.

Eat on the cheap - Febo, Walk to Wok, and Maoz are all inexpensive restaurants. Furthermore, cafes in the city offer prix-fixe lunch deals ranging from 10-15 EUR. Lunch is the finest time to eat out in Amsterdam!

Cook your meals - Dutch cuisine is not going to win any culinary honors, and eating out in the city is costly. Instead, go to the shop and cook your meals. You're not missing out on anything, and you'll save a lot.

Stay with a local - Couchsurfing allows travelers to stay with locals for free. Not only do you get a free place to stay, but you also get to meet a local who can give insider information and advice. Because this service is popular among travelers, place your requests for hosts as soon as possible.

Save money on rideshares - Uber is less expensive than taxis and the ideal method to move around a city if you don't want to wait for a bus or pay for a taxi.

Attend a free festival - During the summer, everyone spends the entire day outside, and there are numerous activities taking place. Check with your local tourism bureau for a list of free concerts, festivals, events, and markets. When the weather warms up, the social calendar fills up, and most of it is free!

Carry a water bottle - The tap water here is safe to drink, so carry a reusable water bottle to save money and decrease your plastic consumption. LifeStraw is my go-to brand since its bottles include built-in filters that keep your water pure and safe.

Visa Requirements (Latest 2024 Update)

Despite what major media sites state, most of our regular readers do not need visas to visit Europe. If you are from the United States, Canada, Australia, the United Kingdom, or any other country, you probably won't need a visa to visit Europe in 2024.

This is why we were left perplexed when Yahoo News headlined: "Americans Will Need A Visa To Visit Europe Beginning In 2024." Here Is What You Should Know.

The first thing you should know is that **you will not need a visa to visit Europe beginning in 2024.** You will need a new travel authorization, as Forbes concisely headlined: "Europe's New Entry Requirements Are No Big Deal."

You'll only need to fill out an online form - something many Europeans have had to do for years when planning trips to the United States - and pay 7 euros.

This is a new requirement under ETIAS, which stands for the European Travel Information and Authorization System. As of this writing, 30 European nations will need visa-exempt tourists, including many of us, to obtain an ETIAS travel authorization before entering.

The application process appears to be quick and simple, but authorities **strongly advise you to obtain the ETIAS travel authorization before you buy your tickets and book your hotels.**

Of course, this is unrealistic for many of us because we need to plan our river trips and flights well in advance. Still, according to ETIAS' official website, (https://travel-europe.europa.eu/etias/faqs-etias_en), "Most applications will be processed within minutes and at the latest within 96 hours." However, some candidates may be required to give extra information or paperwork, or to engage in an interview with national authorities, which might take up to an additional 30 days."

Your travel permission will be connected to your passport and will be valid for up to three years or until the passport expires, whichever occurs first. If you obtain a new passport, you will require a new ETIAS travel permission.

The new online system is not yet operational. What can you do to prepare? Step one is to ensure that your passport is up to date. Most countries would want to **ensure that their passports have at least six months of validity before flying to Europe.** This is what the United States Department of State tells its citizens. If you're traveling with children under the age of 16, make sure to check their passports too. Children's passports are valid for five years, not ten, as is the case for US citizens aged 16 and up.

What are we doing? We're planning our vacation for 2024, including a couple of barge cruises in late April/early May and my Dream Cruise from Amsterdam in October, which brings to mind another erroneous news item reported by major news sites.

Several newspapers have reported in recent weeks that Amsterdam has banned cruise ships from docking there. "Amsterdam Is The Latest European City To Restrict Cruise Ships," according to an August 4, 2023 news story in Minnesota's Star Tribune. Similarly, the tourism industry trade Travelpulse reported: "Amsterdam Bans Cruise Ships from Docking in City." Other major news outlets joined in to cover the prohibition.

The difficulty is that Amsterdam didn't do anything like that. As Condé Nast Traveler rightly reported, Amsterdam has taken a step toward banning cruises. *Voting is complete, but Amsterdam cruises are still available. The future of cruise ships docking in the center of Amsterdam* is still up in the air following the July 20 resolution by the city council of Amsterdam to prohibit cruise ships from operating there.

Indeed, the council's decision to adopt the prohibition was merely a recommendation for action. "There is no immediate closing of the terminal," Dick de Graaff, director of the Amsterdam cruise port, told the Associated Press after the vote on July 20. *The council has called for the terminal to be moved, and we are awaiting an update on the investigation from the alderman.*

We also want to know whether Amsterdam's city council is targeting only huge ocean-going vessels or all ships, including river tours. We do know that Cruise Port Amsterdam has ships planned to dock in the city until well into 2026.

Explore AMSTERDAM | **61**

Transportation Guide

Amsterdam is quite easy to get to, thanks to its well-connected transit options. I will discuss the three most popular ways for people to arrive in the city. Please keep in mind that, if possible, arriving by car or driving is not suggested due to parking issues.

Flying

First and foremost, if you are visiting from overseas, you should book a flight to Amsterdam Airport Schiphol, the city's principal international gateway. When you arrive at Schiphol, you may simply go to the city center by boarding a train from the airport's railway station.

Train

If you're already in Europe and prefer to travel by train, Amsterdam has excellent connections to the European rail network. You can take a high-speed or international train to Amsterdam Central Station.

The train ride can be a lovely way to get into the city, and it's especially useful if you're traveling from adjacent countries such as Belgium, France, or Germany.

Ship Cruise

Finally, many people visit Amsterdam as part of their European cruise. The port is near the train station, and passengers can spend the day touring the city as part of their itinerary.

Ships will sometimes dock in Rotterdam before continuing to Amsterdam by excursions and shuttles.

This is how I got to the city. While my stay was limited, it provided me with an excellent taste of all Amsterdam had to offer, and I am determined to return.

Explore AMSTERDAM | **63**

Explore AMSTERDAM | **64**

Accommodation Options

The city offers a wide selection of housing alternatives to meet a variety of budgets. There are also wheelchair-accessible hotels in Amsterdam to select from. However, these are my top picks.

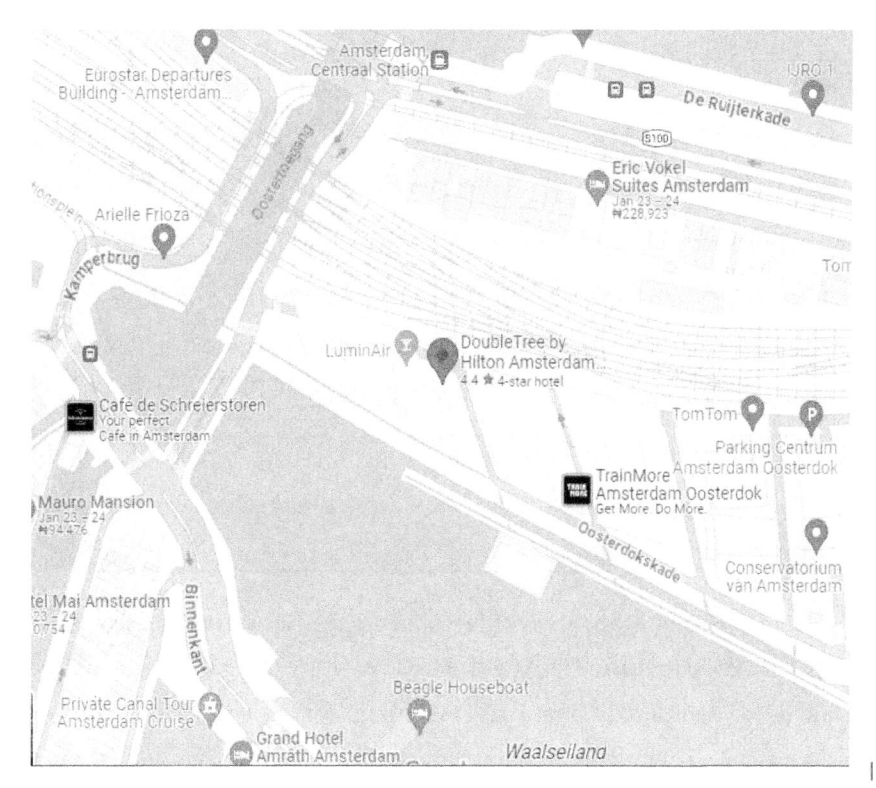

DOUBLETREE BY HILTON HOTEL AMSTERDAM CENTRAAL STATION

This hotel, located near Amsterdam Central Station, stands out as one of the city's most popular. Catering to a wide range of customers, the hotel ensures accessibility for those with disabilities while providing various high-quality amenities.

Notably, booking an accessible room at the **DoubleTree by Hilton Hotel Amsterdam Centraal Station** (http://tinyurl.com/2wtfrc4m) includes additional amenities including fold-down grab bars, wider doorways, an emergency bathroom pull cord, step-free entrances, and accessible public spaces, including handicapped parking.

In addition, each guest room at DoubleTree by Hilton Amsterdam Central Station has floor-to-ceiling windows, a flat-screen TV, and free Wi-Fi, as well as stunning city views. Furthermore, the hotel has pleasant open-air spaces, including a delightful courtyard ideal for leisure.

For tourists looking for convenience, the hotel's location is great, with tram and metro connections nearby. Major sites such as Dam Square are within a 5-minute walk while getting to Amsterdam Schiphol Airport by rail or automobile takes about 20 minutes.

HOLIDAY INN EXPRESS AMSTERDAM, CITY HALL

The Holiday Inn Express rooms are spacious and equipped with important amenities such as a wardrobe, flat-screen TV, and towels. Some rooms also have gorgeous city views, which adds to the ambiance of the stay.

Daily housekeeping services offer a clean and comfortable environment, and guests can begin their day with a continental or vegetarian breakfast served by the hotel. Furthermore, there are several restaurants and a large grocery shop close to the hotel.

For visitors who require accessibility features, the **Holiday Inn Express Amsterdam - City Hall** (http://tinyurl.com/4rme4thk) provides a step-free entrance and in-room amenities designed for convenience. The accessible rooms have bathrooms with a roll-in shower, elevated toilet seat, grab bars, and an emergency pull cord, offering a comfortable and safe stay for all guests.

EUPHEMIA OLD CITY CANAL ZONE

Euphemia Historic City Canal Zone, formerly a historic convent, is a laid-back hotel with a prime central location in Amsterdam. To start the day, you can choose an à la carte breakfast for a few Euros. There is also a vending machine where you can obtain food and hot drinks all day. Their lounge is open from 8:00 a.m. to 11:00 p.m., so you can drop in to meet other travelers, watch TV, or use their free Wi-Fi. If you want to explore the city on pedals, they'd be pleased to arrange a bike rental. There is bike parking directly outside the hostel.

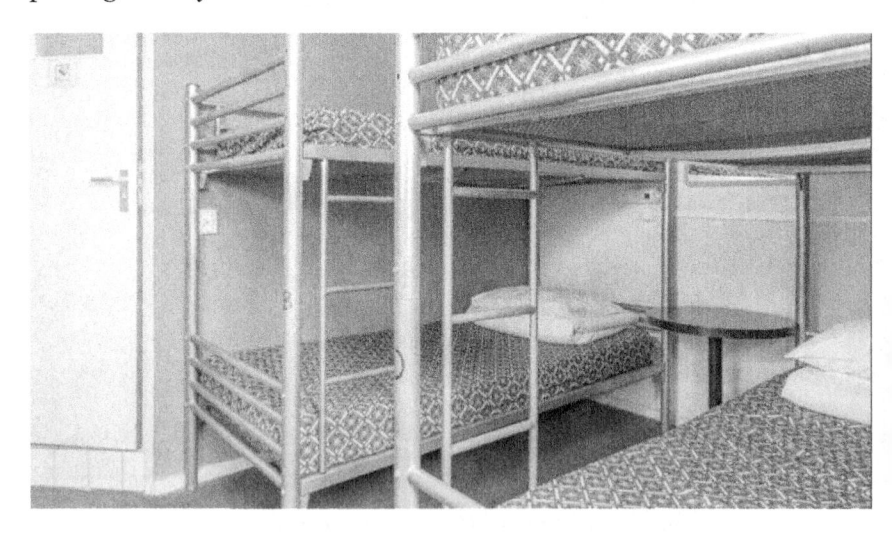

Location: They are close to the city's main attractions, such as the Heineken Brewery and Museum Quarter (a must-see), Leidseplein Square, and the Anne Frank House. Despite their proximity to some of the city's top nightspots, they are located on a quiet side street, so noise should not disturb your sleep. To get to the hostel from the airport, take the train to Amsterdam Central Station, then Metro # 52 to Wijzelgracht. The Fokke Simonszstraat is located on the left side of the roadway. Alternatively, Bus 397 from the airport will take you to the Rijksmuseum, from which it is a 10-minute walk.

They provide private rooms of various sizes. They're located over four levels (no lift). All the rooms have private bathrooms; all 2 and 3-person rooms have towels in the room; 4 and 5-person rooms can rent a towel at reception for €1.00.

Extras and Activities: You'll find plenty of useful accessories, such as adapters. If you want to relax, take advantage of their book exchange. When you're ready to continue your journey, they'll gladly store your bags before you fly.

Hostel conditions:

Credit cards: Please ensure your credit card has enough funds to cover the entire reservation cost or authorization. If they are unable to charge or authorize the credit card, the reservation may be canceled. You may pay at the hotel with debit cards, however, they do not take any sort of debit/VISA debit for online reservations.

The credit card used for the reservation, as well as the cardholder, must be present at the time of arrival; otherwise, they may cancel the credit card charge and require you to pay in cash or with another present card.

During the stay, they may also require a security deposit ranging from €50 to €100.

There is a 5% extra if you pay with a credit or debit card at the hotel.

Non-refundable rate reservations: For non-refundable reservations, they will charge the credit card the entire cost minus HostelWorld's commission, plus local tax and tourist fees (€3 per person per night).

There is no compensation for cancellations or modifications made before or after arrival, or for no-shows.

For standard rate reservations: They will authorize the credit card for the total room price minus the fee paid to HostelWorld. Please note that the City Tax (7%) and Tourist Fee (€3, per person per night) are not included in their rates and will be added upon arrival.

Authorization means they request that your credit card company block an amount (often equal to the cancellation charge).

This amount is generally valid for a few weeks before being automatically released back into your account (depending on the credit card provider and country); after arrival, you can utilize this authorization as part of the payment; they do not influence the release process.

To cancel, please send an email to the hotel 48 hours before the arrival date, not the arrival time.

Failure to do so will result in a 100% charge for the total amount. Cancellations and modifications made on or after the arrival date will incur a 100% charge.

Groups: No parties! STAG/HEN/BACHELOR PARTY GROUPS are not permitted; this type of reservation will be declined.

For group reservations (10 or more people), they have separate policies and additional supplements.

Non-Smoking! At Euphemia, smoking and vaping are not permitted anywhere! Smoking in the Euphemia, activating the smoke alarm, causing any other damage, or covering the smoke detector, will result in a charge of €.100.

Check-in: Check-in is only permitted between 08.00 am and 11.00 pm, and rooms are available beginning at 2.00 pm.

If you arrive early, they have a storage area. If you arrive after 23:00, please call us to arrange an after-hours entry.

At check-in, they will provide you with key cards for your accommodation; a €.10 deposit is required per key card.

Check-out: Reception opens at 08.00 AM. If you need to check out sooner then, please make arrangements the night before by 10.30 PM.

The check-out time is at 10 a.m. Extensions will be offered based on availability. Failure to quit the room will result in management removing the guest and his/her possessions from the room occupied by the guest and charging additional fees equal to the hotel payment for the day.

Guest's Belongings: To protect their belongings, guests should lock their room doors upon leaving. Lockers are available in the room for the guests' convenience. It is strongly advised to keep all valuable items in the safe deposit box at the reception. The management shall not be held liable for any loss or damage to the guest's goods or other property from the hotel room, locker, or any other portion of the hotel, for any reason whatsoever.

Damage to Property: Visitors are responsible for any damage or loss to hotel property caused by themselves, their visitors, or anybody they are responsible for.

Management's Rights: Guests must conduct themselves respectfully and refrain from causing any nuisance or inconvenience within the hotel premises. No parties of any kind, including sleepovers, are permitted at the hotel.

I wish you a pleasant visit.

MEININGER AMSTERDAM CITY WEST

Welcome to MEININGER Hotel Amsterdam City West! The hotel is located about two minutes from the Sloterdijk train station and a few minutes by rail from the airport. The rooms are comfortable, clean, and reasonably priced; everything you'll need for a visit to Amsterdam.

Hotel Location: The MEININGER Hotel Amsterdam City West is located in Sloterdijk, a neighborhood within the Westpoort district. Their hotel is ideally positioned near the Sloterdijk train station. From there, it's only one train stop to Central Station and ten minutes to Schiphol Airport. Everything is at your fingertips.

Explore the Meininger Hotel Amsterdam City West: The MEININGER Hotel Amsterdam City West's foyer immediately immerses you in the realm of the Old Masters. The modern decor was influenced by Vincent van Gogh's colors and shapes. In their fully equipped guest kitchen, you may prepare a delicious meal for yourself and your friends. Their bar serves local beers and delicacies, as well as hot appetizers if you're hungry. In their game zone, you can play pool or table football with new acquaintances. The warm alternative: you can put your feet up in their lobby and talk with your loved ones. Free WiFi is available in all public spaces and rooms.

Rooms—Everything You Need: Beds are available in either single, twin, or multi-bedded rooms. There is a TV, plugs, and reading lights near the beds, as well as lockers and a clothes rack in the rooms. All rooms feature an en suite bathroom with a shower, toilet, and complimentary toiletries.

Their young, international welcome team is always delighted to assist you and is available 24 hours a day, seven days a week. Come over and say hello; they'll help you organize your day!

Public Areas:

- Lounge

- Lobby

- Bar

- Game zone

- Children area

- Fully equipped kitchen

- Accessible public areas

Free Services:

- 24h reception

- High-speed Wi-Fi available in all areas

- Bedding

- Towels (excluding dorms)

- City maps

- Use of guest kitchen

- Baby cots (subject to availability)

Services Available for A Small Fee:

- Breakfast buffet

- Packed lunch

- Towels to rent

- Washer & dryer

- Rental bikes

- Luggage lockers

- Public transport tickets

- Tickets for city tours, musicals, etc.

- Vending machine (snacks & drinks)

- Late check-out (for private rooms only) until 2:00 PM

- Pets are welcome (only in private rooms)

- Parking spots

HOSTEL VAN GOGH

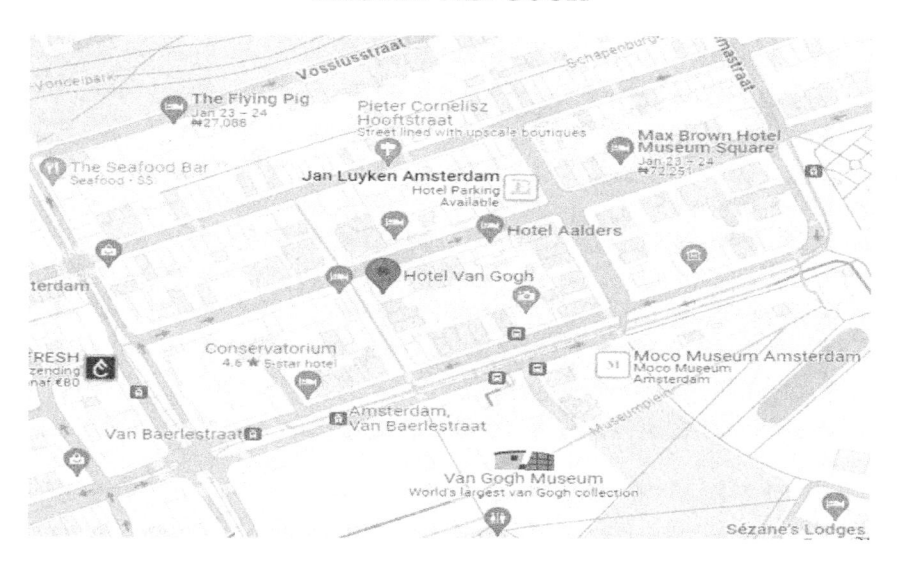

If you want to visit museums while in Amsterdam, Hostel Van Gogh is in an excellent position, near the Van Gogh Museum and the Rijksmuseum. It's also a terrific place to unwind, with Vondelpark and the nightlife of Leidseplein just a short walk away. Their reviewers say that this clean, modern, and "easily accessible" hostel is evocative of a hotel, and they recommend it for travelers who "appreciate calmness and cleanliness but don't want to pay hotel rates."

Property Description: This new youth accommodation, located between Vondel Park and the Van Gogh Museum, is one of the best in Amsterdam Center!!

Museums At Your Door: The Van Gogh Museum, the Rijksmuseum, and the Stedelijk Art Museum are three of the most important and well-known museums in the world, all of which are conveniently close to Hostel Van Gogh. The hostel is situated in the most desirable area of Amsterdam's Museum District, directly across from the Van Gogh Museum, the city's center for art, fashion, and culture.

Quality And Modern: Hostel Van Gogh offers high-quality facilities and modern rooms with private bathrooms. Designed to meet the needs of youthful travelers who place minimal value on comfort and quality. The entire property is centrally air-conditioned, and each room has an LCD television and a modern bathroom with a hairdryer. The hostel offers free bed linen, shampoo, and shower gel, free luggage storage, a lift, and an all-you-can-eat continental breakfast buffet for €10.

Free Towel, Free Wi-Fi, Mini Fridge, And More: They provide a complimentary towel for each visitor and free wifi throughout the accommodation. If you like a little extra luxury, the Twin/Triple/Quad Private Rooms include a mini fridge, Nespresso machine, and tea maker.

Entertaining Zone: Leidseplein

The hostel is conveniently located near many of the city's bars, shops, clubs, and other attractions. If you enjoy the thrilling nightlife, the entertainment district Leidseplein is only a five-minute walk away.

No curfew and high security: There's no curfew. Guests can enter at any time with their key card, and there is security staff available at night to assist them. Each bed has its safety box for storing valuables or laptops.

VAT of 9% is included. From January 2020, the new city tax will be 7%, payable at check-in. Guests above the age of 16 must pay an additional tax of 3 euros per person per night upon arrival.

The hostel-shared dorm room check-in desk shuts from noon to midnight. If you book dorm beds and plan to arrive after this hour, they are unable to accommodate you. If you reserved a private room, please check in with security and be quiet.

This hostel does not offer a dedicated bike parking area, and bikes are not permitted to be carried into the hostel!

STAYOKAY AMSTERDAM VONDELPARK

Stayokay Amsterdam Vondelpark is located near the Van Gogh Museum, the Rijksmuseum, and the nightlife on Leidseplein, with a view of Vondelpark however, there are various buses and trams nearby that travel across the city. According to Hostelworld guests, this hostel provides excellent value for money and is a good fit for foreign visitors. And that they would recommend it? Do you wish to spend a quiet night in Amsterdam? They particularly enjoy their well-known, quintessentially Dutch breakfast of cheese, meats, eggs, and more.

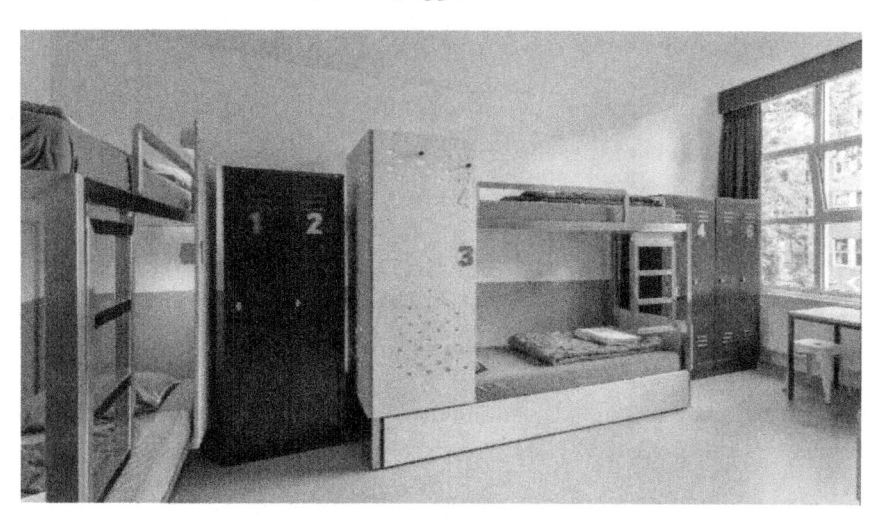

Property Description:

Stay in Amsterdam's green core to experience the true essence of the city. Consume culture, shop till you drop, and party the night away in Amsterdam. Stayokay Amsterdam Vondelpark is the ideal starting place! This new Hostelling International hostel is centrally positioned in the heart of the famed Vondelpark, just a short walk from the Van Gogh and Rijksmuseum. They're just a short walk from the famous nightlife district of Leidseplein, which includes clubs like Paradiso, Melkweg, and Jimmy Woo.

The hostel is partly housed in a historic chalet building with a spectacular view of Vondelpark! They have 574 beds divided into two-, four--, six-, and eight-bed rooms, as well as several large dormitories. One room is wheelchair accessible (please request before booking). All rooms include a shower, toilet, and washbasin, as well as complimentary individual lockers (bring your padlock or purchase one at reception). Other amenities include a lobby area, free Wi-Fi, a laundromat, a bike shelter, tourist information and discounted tickets, electronic door locks, lockers, and safes. Their reception is open 24 hours a day, seven days a week, with no curfew.

Their bustling bar features sports on television and fantastic music. You will meet many folks here. They serve hearty and healthful meals at reasonable prices, and their beer is the lowest in town.

At the reception, you may get discounted tickets for a variety of Amsterdam attractions (Museums, Canal Tour, Heineken Experience, Madame Tussauds).

That's good to know!

- Breakfast is not included, but can be booked individually or purchased at the hostel. Breakfast is € 9.95.

- You will be given bed linen upon arrival so that you can make your bed. Towels are NOT included. These can be rented from the hostel for € 3.50 per towel.

- Padlocks for luggage lockers are available for purchase at the desk (or bring your own).

- Standard rooms include bunk beds.

- Guests under the age of 16 must be accompanied by their parents or legal guardians. Please read their Things to Remember section before booking.

-A tourist tax of 12.5% per night of the accommodation rate is not included. Please pay upon arrival.

- Stayokay and Hostelling International members do not receive a discount on this reservation.

Stayokay Amsterdam Vondelpark is a cashless hostel. You can pay with all major bank and credit cards, including contactless payments. They do not accept cash payments in their accommodations.

THE FLYING PIG DOWNTOWN

Hostelworld users routinely praise Flying Pig Downtown's high degree of cleanliness as well as its staff, which one of their visitors described as *adorable, very friendly, talkative, helpful, and always in a good mood.* They loved this hostel's central position in Amsterdam, around ten minutes from Centraal Station - *which was easy to get to from the airport,* making it the *perfect way to experience everything Amsterdam has to offer.* Reviewers say this is a wonderful spot to meet other tourists because *people are usually hanging out at the bar, playing pool, or socializing.*

Property Description:

Do you want to hang out at one of the most famous hostel bars, which includes an indoor smoking area and a pillow stage?

The Flying Pig Downtown is the place to be, just opposite Amsterdam Central Station.

They provide dorms with reading lights on each bed, as well as individual rooms with a small refrigerator and television. The rates include free linen. Most rooms include single and queen-size bunk beds, as well as a shower and toilet. There are also complimentary individual lockers in the rooms; bring your padlock or purchase one at reception for only 5 EUR.

The Flying Pig Downtown offers free use of the guest kitchen, luggage storage, free Wi-Fi, a book exchange, and a busy hostel bar with DJ nights and the cheapest beer around. A continental breakfast is served every morning for €7 per day and may be purchased at reception upon arrival.

This hostel makes it simple to meet new people while relaxing on lounge pillows in the smoking area, drinking and playing pool in the bar, dancing to local DJs' music, and cooking meals in the guest kitchen.

They are open 24 hours a day with keycard access to the hostel, and there is no curfew or lockout. You can store modest items in the safe behind reception. Their front desk provides excursions and tickets to Amsterdam's sights, as well as Piggy merchandise.

They provide a free walking tour that picks up visitors from the hostel every day, a daily updated Amsterdam agenda, a free thorough map of Amsterdam, and discounts on various activities in the city.

The accommodation rate does not include the 12.5% city tax, which will be added to your balance.

This is a government requirement with which they must comply.

Leaving Central Station, it is only a five-minute walk to the hostel, and you will instantly see several restaurants, pubs, red lights from the famous Red

Light District, and shops. That is the party zone where you will most likely spend your nights.

The hostel entrance is on Amsterdam's biggest retail street, making it an ideal site to begin your night of club, pub, and coffee shop hopping. Aside from everything the hostel has to offer, their international Piggy staff can provide you with all of the information you need to make the most of your Amsterdam experience.

The Red Light District, with its famed windows, is conveniently located near their accommodation. Walking about here is fairly safe, and it's a great spot to hang out at night. There's also Anne Frank House, which transports you back to the Second World War. In this house, Anne Frank and her family hid for years before being transported to a concentration camp. The Royal Palace is very impressive, with its magnificent 16th-century halls and apartments, as is Dam Square, which hosts musical groups, performers, and other entertainers.

Please keep in mind that they do not host guests under the age of 18, and photo identification is requested at check-in.

Valid passports or national ID cards are acceptable; driver's licenses are not.

Explore AMSTERDAM | **82**

Must-Visit Attractions

Amsterdam is one of Europe's most popular—and accessible—cities, with Golden Age canals, remarkable 17th-century architecture, culture-filled museums, and lovely parks, all connected by cycle-friendly streets and tulip-laden bridges. A canal boat trip is one of the nicest things to do in Amsterdam, even though much of the Dutch capital's highlights are easily accessible by foot. Although the Rijksmuseum and Anne Frank House are must-sees, the entire city feels like an open-air museum, so set aside plenty of time to explore the winding streets and chocolate-box architecture.

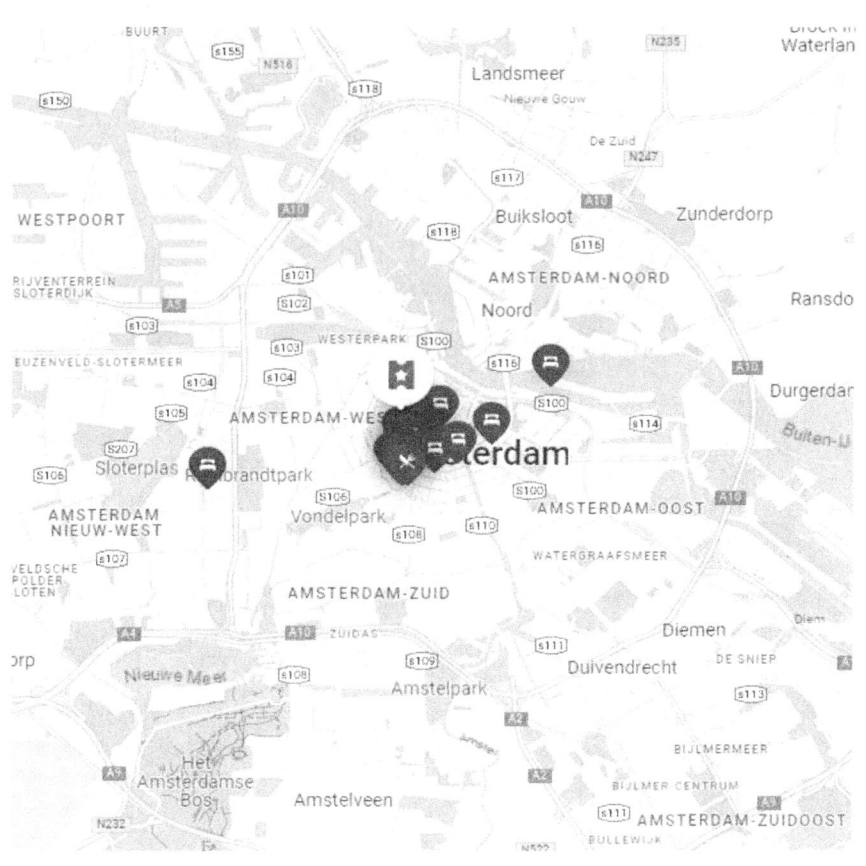

See Anne Frank House

This is one of the most visited tourist attractions in the entire city. It is the house where Anne Frank and her family hid during World War II, and the attic depicts her childhood and existence. Her handwritten diary is also on view. While it's a significant and tragic location to visit, it's also extremely crowded. You just shuffle through the house, never having time to process what you're seeing. I believe the Jewish History Museum does a better job of showcasing her life, but it is still worth visiting because it is such an iconic and significant site.

The museum is normally rather packed, so if you want a more in-depth experience, joining this Anne Frank walking tour is a fantastic alternative because it provides a lot more background into Anne Frank's period and what the city was like during the occupation.

Prinsengracht 263-267, +31 20 556 71 05; annefrank.org. Open every day from 9 a.m. to 10 p.m. Admission costs 16 EUR. Tickets are only available online.

Visit the Van Gogh Museum

This museum houses several of Van Gogh's best paintings. It also houses the world's greatest collection of Van Gogh artwork. The museum does an outstanding job of summarizing his life and work from beginning to conclusion, allowing you to better comprehend and appreciate his style and evolution. It opened in 1973 and is now one of the city's most popular (read: crowded) attractions, but don't let that deter you from coming. The museum also houses paintings by other well-known artists of the time, such as Monet, Manet, and Matisse, as well as works by artists who influenced or were inspired by Van Gough.

Museumplein 6, +31 20 570 5200; vangoghmuseum.nl. Summer hours are 9 a.m. to 6 p.m., with reduced hours in the spring, fall, and winter. Book your ticket ahead of time to avoid the extremely long lines! (http://tinyurl.com/4afc6rfr) Admission costs 22 EUR.

Visit the Rijksmuseum

The Rijksmuseum, founded in 1798, is an art and history museum located adjacent to the Van Gogh Museum. The substantially rebuilt museum houses an extensive Rembrandt collection, including the iconic picture "The Night Watch." In addition to Rembrandt's paintings, the museum houses a large collection of other famous Dutch painters such as Frans Hals and Johannes Vermeer. The collection contains about 1 million objects (it is the largest museum in the country), with over 8,000 on display, so you could easily spend a few hours there.

Museumstraat 1, +31 20 674 7000; rijksmuseum.nl. Open everyday from 9 a.m. to 5 p.m. Admission costs 22.50 EUR.

Explore Jordaan

Jordaan is a stylish residential neighborhood. Despite its growing popularity in recent years, it remains one of the city's most ignored areas. The area is brimming with charming stores and boutiques, bars and taverns, and trendy eateries. It is also the neighborhood where the Dutch painter Rembrandt (1606-1669) spent his last years. It's a peaceful place to explore away from the throng if you want to get a better sense of the city outside of the popular tourist sites.

In addition to eating and drinking, you may shop at the Westerstraat Market (Monday mornings) and the Lindengracht Market (Saturdays).

Relax in Vondelpark

This park, established in 1865, is Amsterdam's largest (and most popular). It spans 120 acres and is ideal for walking, biking, people-watching, or relaxing, especially after a visit to a nearby coffee shop. In the summer, the park is bustling with activity, and there are frequently numerous events held here. Pack a picnic lunch, bring a book, and enjoy a beautiful afternoon!

Try the Heineken Experience

Heineken is one of the most well-known (and popular) beers in the world. Take an interactive self-guided tour of this former brewery to learn about how the beer was manufactured and how the company changed over time (the beer dates back to the 1870s). Admission includes two beers, so if you're a fan, make sure you schedule a tour. It's a wonderful approach to learning about history.

A combination ticket for both the Heineken experience and the canal cruise is also available online (http://tinyurl.com/ms97jn5p).

Stadhouderskade 78, +31 020 261 1323; heinekenexperience.com. Monday through Thursday and Sunday from 10:30 a.m. to 7:30 p.m.; Friday and Saturday from 10:30 a.m. to 9:00 p. Admission costs 23 EUR.

Our Lord in the Attic Museum Ons' Lieve Heer op Solder

Hidden amid Amsterdam's city center sits a modest wonder: Our Lord in the Attic Museum. Visitors will go on a tour of a fascinating, well-preserved canal house from the seventeenth century. Narrow passageways and steps lead to historically adorned living quarters, kitchens, and bedsteads, culminating in the museum's true highlight: a fully functional church in the attic.

The area: Oudezijds Voorburgwal 38-40, 1012 GD Amsterdam. The Netherlands

Neighborhood: Centrum

Amsterdam's thriving core, with its huge tram-train network and continual flow of tourists and commuters, provides easy access to some of Europe's best sightseeing, shopping, and street culture. The Royal Palace, the charming shops of Haalremmerdijk, the pedestrianized zones Kalverstraat and Dam Square, as well as popular areas like the Red Light District and the Canal Ring, are all within easy reach. Centrum's basis is the well-connected Centraal Station, from where you may easily go further afield on one of the city's famed trams.

Directions: Centraal Station is a 4-minute walk away.

Nieuwmarkt • 5 minute walk

Reach out directly (https://opsolder.nl/)

Centraal Station

P.J.H. Cuypers, who also created the famed Rijksmuseum, designed this neo-Renaissance rail station, which was completed in 1889 and is located in the middle of town.

The area: Stationsplein 9, 1012 AB Amsterdam. The Netherlands.

Neighborhood is Centrum

Amsterdam's thriving core, with its huge tram-train network and continual flow of tourists and commuters, provides easy access to some of Europe's best sightseeing, shopping, and street culture. The Royal Palace, the charming shops of Haalremmerdijk, the pedestrianized zones Kalverstraat and Dam Square, as well as popular areas like the Red Light District and the Canal Ring, are all within easy reach. Centrum's basis is the well-connected Centraal Station, from where you may easily go further afield on one of the city's famed trams.

How to Get There

Amsterdam Centraal Station • 2-minute walk

Amsterdam Centraal • 2-minute walk

Reach out directly: (https://www.gvb.nl/)

Red Light District

Amsterdam's De Wallen neighborhood is home to one of the world's most famous red light districts. Take a walk to enjoy the rousing yet beautiful lights, or visit the Red Lights Secrets Museum to discover more about Amsterdam's sex work industry. The area is also famous for its fashionable coffee shops, pubs, and clubs.

The best time to visit the region is in the early evening or at night when the lights start to illuminate the small streets. The place is safe, but it can get crowded, and taking photos or films of workers is prohibited.

Neighborhood: Centrum.

Amsterdam's thriving core, with its huge tram-train network and continual flow of tourists and commuters, provides easy access to some of Europe's best sightseeing, shopping, and street culture. The Royal Palace, the charming shops of Haalremmerdijk, the pedestrianized zones Kalverstraat and Dam Square, as well as popular areas like the Red Light District and the Canal Ring, are all within easy reach. Centrum's basis is the well-connected Centraal Station, from where you may easily go further afield on one of the city's famed trams.

How to Get There

Walking distances: 3 minutes to Nieuwmarkt and 7 minutes to Centraal Station.

Verzetmuseum Amsterdam

Discover the genuine experiences and fates of ordinary people during World War II in the Netherlands. What did life seem like? What decisions did you have to make? Travel back in time with the Resistance Museum.

The area: Plantage Kerklaan 61, 1018 CX Amsterdam. The Netherlands

Neighborhood: Centrum

Amsterdam's thriving core, with its huge tram-train network and continual flow of tourists and commuters, provides easy access to some of Europe's best sightseeing, shopping, and street culture. The Royal Palace, the charming shops of Haalremmerdijk, the pedestrianized zones Kalverstraat and Dam Square, as well as popular areas like the Red Light District and the Canal Ring, are all within easy reach. Centrum's basis is the well-connected Centraal Station, from where you may easily go further afield on one of the city's famed trams.

How to Get There

Waterlooplein • 10-minute walk.

Weesperplein • 10-minute walk.

Contact them directly (https://www.verzetsmuseum.org/).

Reach out directly: (https://www.verzetsmuseum.org/)

Body Worlds

Gunther von Hagens' BODY WORLDS: The Happiness Project, located in the center of Amsterdam, presents the incredible story of our bodies and the impact of happiness on health. More than 200 anatomical specimens of genuine human bodies demonstrate the intricacy, resilience, and vulnerability of the body. Join the 40 million individuals worldwide who have already seen the exhibition and embarked on this exciting journey of discovery through the human body.

The area: Damrak 66; 1012 LM Amsterdam. The Netherlands

Damrak neighborhood

How to Get There

Centraal Station is within a 7-minute walk away, as is Nieuwmarkt.

Contact us personally: (https://www.bodyworlds.nl/en/).

ARTIS Amsterdam Royal Zoo

Stroll amid the shady trees, see the diversity of plants and animals, journey to the heavens, and celebrate our heritage. Visit the ARTIS Amsterdam Royal Zoo to discover nature right in the city center.

The area: Plantage Kerklaan 38-40, 1018 CZ. Amsterdam The Netherlands

Neighborhood: Centrum

Amsterdam's thriving core, with its huge tram-train network and continual flow of tourists and commuters, provides easy access to some of Europe's best sightseeing, shopping, and street culture. The Royal Palace, the charming shops of Haalremmerdijk, the pedestrianized zones Kalverstraat and Dam Square, as well as popular areas like the Red Light District and the Canal Ring, are all within easy reach. Centrum's basis is the well-connected Centraal Station, from where you may easily go further afield on one of the city's famed trams.

How to Get There

Weesperplein • 9-minute walk.

Waterlooplein • 10-minute walk.

Contact them directly (https://www.artis.nl/en/).

Museum Het Rembrandthuis

From 1639 to 1658, Rembrandt lived and worked in this 17th-century house, which is now a museum commemorating the artist's life and career.

The area: Jodenbreestraat 4, 1011 NK Amsterdam. The Netherlands

Neighborhood: Centrum

Amsterdam's thriving core, with its huge tram-train network and continual flow of tourists and commuters, provides easy access to some of

Europe's best sightseeing, shopping, and street culture. The Royal Palace, the charming shops of Haalremmerdijk, the pedestrianized zones Kalverstraat and Dam Square, as well as popular areas like the Red Light District and the Canal Ring, are all within easy reach. Centrum's basis is the well-connected Centraal Station, from where you may easily go further afield on one of the city's famed trams.

How to Get There

Waterlooplein • 3-minute walk.

Four-minute walk to Nieuwmarkt.

Contact us directly (https://www.rembrandthuis.nl/?lang=en).

Concertgebouw

The Royal Concertgebouw is one of the world's most famous music halls, known for its excellent acoustics. With 700 events per year, the Concertgebouw presents a diverse schedule comprising top international soloists, orchestras, and conductors. The hall serves as the home base for the Royal Concertgebouw Orchestra, one of the top orchestras in the world. Critics have often praised its distinct sound, which distinguishes it from countless other recordings. Behind-the-scenes excursions offer insight into the performance hall's fascinating history. Tours are held three times a week and are available for groups upon request. From September to June, 12:30 pm. Every Wednesday, there is a free 30-minute concert at the Concertgebouw. Due to the popularity of these concerts, it is recommended that you arrive at least 45 minutes early.

The area: Concertgebouwplein 10, Museum Quarter, 1071 LN Amsterdam. The Netherlands

Neighborhood: Museum Quarter (Museumkwartier).

The Rijksmuseum and the Van Gogh Museum are two of the widely acclaimed institutions in the aptly titled Museum Quarter. If you need a break from all the amazing art, visit the Neoclassical Concertgebouw music hall and Vondelpark, the city's largest park. Shopaholics and luxury brand enthusiasts will enjoy exploring the high-end retail areas of PC Hooftstraat, Van Baerlestraat, Cornelis Schuytstraat, and Jacob Obrechtstraat, where even the shop window displays are museum-quality. When the museums close and the daytrippers leave, the region transforms into a tranquil haven with a refined and urbane vibe.

Contact them personally (https://www.concertgebouw.nl/en).

A'dam Lookout

LOOKOUT: 360° Amsterdam + amazing Swing A'DAM LOOKOUT, an iconic observation point in the Netherlands, has joined the Eiffel Tower, Fernsehturm, and London Eye. For the daredevils among us, LOOKOUT has an additional adrenaline boost in store. On the roof stands Europe's tallest swing. You hang over the brink of the tower at a thrilling height of about 100 meters above the ground. Highlights: - The most stunning perspective of Amsterdam and the surrounding area - A bird's-eye view of Amsterdam from Europe's highest swing - Access to the indoor interactive state-of-the-art Amsterdam exhibition. - Free digital photo of your visit to LOOKOUT - Enjoy coffee, breakfast, lunch, dinner, and/or cocktails at Madam Restaurant & Sky Bar - Free WIFI available Only card payments are accepted.

The area: Overhoeksplein 5, 1031 KS Amsterdam. The Netherlands

Neighborhood: Noordelijke IJ-oevers.

How to Get There: Amsterdam Centraal Station • A 7-minute stroll to Amsterdam Centraal.

Contact them personally (https://www.adamlookout.com/).

Dam Square

All roads lead to Dam Square, the true heart of Amsterdam, where the Royal Palace, the Nieuwe Kerk, and the War Memorial watch over this enormous and vibrant open space.

The area

Neighborhood: Burgwallen-Nieuwe Zijde

How to Get There

Nieuwmarkt • 8-minute walk • 10-minute walk from Central Station.

Contact: (https://www.amsterdam.info/sights/dam_square/).

Moco Museum, Amsterdam

This independent museum in Amsterdam's Museumplein is popular among young people and is dedicated to modern, contemporary, and street art.

The area

(Museumplein) Honthorststraat 20 adjacent to Van Gogh Museum, 1071 DE Amsterdam The Netherlands

Neighborhood: Museum Quarter (Museumkwartier).

The Rijksmuseum and the Van Gogh Museum are two of the widely acclaimed institutions in the aptly titled Museum Quarter. If you need a break from all the amazing art, visit the Neoclassical Concertgebouw music hall and Vondelpark, the city's largest park. Shopaholics and luxury brand enthusiasts will enjoy exploring the high-end retail areas of PC Hooftstraat, Van Baerlestraat, Cornelis Schuytstraat, and Jacob

Obrechtstraat, where even the shop window displays are museum-quality. When the museums close and the daytrippers leave, the region transforms into a tranquil haven with a refined and urbane vibe.

Contact them personally (https://mocomuseum.com/).

The Amsterdam Dungeon

The Amsterdam Dungeon brings 500 years of history to life in about 80 minutes. Meet our witch hunter, soul merchant, and many other mouth breathers while you go deep into the dungeon with (max.) 29 other sinners but you are part of the show (or push another victim forward). Scary true stories and 'horrible actors. English is spoken, but also available in Dutch. If you want to brag. * Ten years or younger? We wouldn't do that, but that's just advice. * Don't tell anyone, but you can leave if you can't handle it any longer.

The area

Rokin 78, 1012 KW Amsterdam.

The Netherlands' neighborhood is Centrum

Amsterdam's thriving core, with its huge tram-train network and continual flow of tourists and commuters, provides easy access to some of Europe's best sightseeing, shopping, and street culture. The Royal Palace, the charming shops of Haalremmerdijk, the pedestrianized zones Kalverstraat and Dam Square, as well as popular areas like the Red-Light District and the Canal Ring, are all within easy reach. Centrum's basis is the well-connected Centraal Station, from where you may easily go further afield on one of the city's famed trams.

How to Get There

Nieuwmarkt • 8-minute walk

Waterlooplein • 10-minute walk.

Contact us personally (https://www.thedungeons.com/amsterdam/).

Het Scheepvaartmuseum | The National Maritime Museum

The National Marine Museum houses one of the world's most extensive and significant marine collections, which includes artworks, ship models, navigation tools, and sea maps. Discover 500 years of Dutch maritime history, as well as its significant connection to modern and future society.

The area

Kattenburgerplein 1, 1018 KK Amsterdam. The Netherlands

Neighborhood: Centrum

Amsterdam's thriving core, with its huge tram-train network and continual flow of tourists and commuters, provides easy access to some of Europe's best sightseeing, shopping, and street culture. The Royal Palace, the charming shops of Haalremmerdijk, the pedestrianized zones

Kalverstraat and Dam Square, as well as popular areas like the Red Light District and the Canal Ring, are all within easy reach. Centrum's basis is the well-connected Centraal Station, from where you may easily go further afield on one of the city's famed trams.

Contact personally (https://www.hetscheepvaartmuseum.com/).

Royal Palace Amsterdam

The Royal Palace Amsterdam is used by the Dutch Royal House. Most of the year, the Royal Palace is also open to visitors. You are invited to explore the rich history and interior of this spectacular edifice in the heart of Amsterdam. Visitors are welcome to learn about the building's rich history and the legacy left by its previous occupants, including Amsterdam's Town Hall for 150 years, the French Royal and Imperial Palace for 5 years, and the Palace of the House of Orange for the last two centuries. Jacob van Campen designed the Royal Palace, which was originally built as Amsterdam's Town Hall, in the seventeenth century. Its paintings and sculptures were created by some of the most renowned artists of the time and reflect the city's importance and affluence during the Dutch Golden Age. Louis Napoleon, the brother of the French Emperor Napoleon Bonaparte, became King of Holland in 1808 and turned the Town Hall into a palace. The magnificent collection of Empire furniture, clocks, and chandeliers dates from that era. The Empire furniture collection is one of the most well-preserved and complete in the world. The Palace's chambers are furnished with artworks from the House of Orange-Nassau Historic Collections Trust. Many artworks depict the many members of the family of Orange-Nassau.

The area

Nieuwezijds Voorburgwal 147, 1012 RJ Amsterdam. Burgwallen-Nieuwe Zijde neighborhood is located in the Netherlands.

How to get there: Neumarkt • 9-minute walk • 10-minute walk to Central Station.

Contact them personally (https://www.paleisamsterdam.nl/).

Experiencing Amsterdam Culture

Welcome to a city where the vivid hues of tulips are mirrored in the many colors of its cultural canvas—Amsterdam, a destination for visitors seeking an authentic, immersive engagement with the arts, traditions, and flavors that distinguish this captivating metropolis.

In this chapter, we invite you to go beyond the postcard-perfect sights and dig into the rich fabric of Amsterdam culture. Join us on a journey that goes beyond the typical tourist experience, from culinary delights to centuries-old customs that echo through cobblestone alleyways. It's time to embrace Amsterdam's cultural lifeblood and make experiences that will last long after you stay.

Best Places to Eat in Amsterdam

Amsterdam has a lot to offer, including sunny lunches on a balcony, tranquil mornings over the canals, and picture-perfect moments everywhere you look. Amsterdam's broad and rich culture ensures that you can find any cuisine you wish.

In this guide, we'll show you some must-see attractions in the city center. Here are our top suggestions for the best Amsterdam eateries.

Nomad Aan Het IJ

Nomad was one of the most enjoyable eating experiences I had in Amsterdam. They've built an extraordinarily sophisticated restaurant and setting, as well as a rotating menu of international fare, which added to the overall enjoyment of the experience—something our party loved.

Furthermore, this restaurant has the nicest ground-level sea views we observed in Amsterdam. A five-course meal with wine pairings costs between €80 and €100, which seemed reasonable. The owners are intimately involved in the day-to-day business, as is the chef from Slovakia. If you have a good travel budget, this is a must-see destination.

Address: Ijdok 87

The Chicken Bar

I did not expect the Chicken Bar to satisfy my expectations, and I was correct. This place far exceeded my expectations for chicken. Boyd Baptist has transformed rotisserie chicken in Amsterdam, making it a must.

The atmosphere is equally as impressive as the food and service. It's fantastic for lunch, but make sure to arrive early or make a reservation! This fashionable cafe is a popular option.

Address: Voetboogstraat 6

O Bistro

O Bistro is owned and operated by a French chef with an Italian front-of-house, which is likely the ideal match. The chef combines foods from his youth that are simply excellent.

When I was there, I had the mackerel, although their menu changes seasonally according to what ingredients are available. Before you order, ask Daniele for recommendations!

Address: Lindengracht 248

Benji's

We stopped in at Benji's after a late night out with some friends, and it treated our hangovers similarly to hot yoga, but without the perspiration. This eatery is extremely well done and serves high-quality meals.

I recommend ordering the Salmon Avocado Toast or simply asking the waiter what you should try. Try ordering something out of your comfort zone because this eatery has some amazing meals.

Address: Three locations

Dignita Hoftuin

What better way to start your first morning in Amsterdam than with a tasty brunch? Dignita Hoftuin, located in the heart of the city, is a hidden gem that serves an all-day breakfast with a stunning green garden and a variety of vegan and vegetarian alternatives!

Eat to your heart's content! You'll not only eat well but also feel great. Dignita Hoftuin is well-known for its courteous service, interesting environment, and wonderful cuisine.

Address: Nieuwe Herengracht 18A.

Mama Makan

Want to experience a flavor of Bali while visiting Amsterdam? Then, travel to Mama Makan in the Plantage area for real Indonesian cuisine with powerful spices. Treat yourself to an excellent Thai experience where you can relax and enjoy Indonesian food, herbal cocktails, and great service.

Address: Spinozastraat 61

Mondi Caribbean Cuisine Restaurant and Terrace

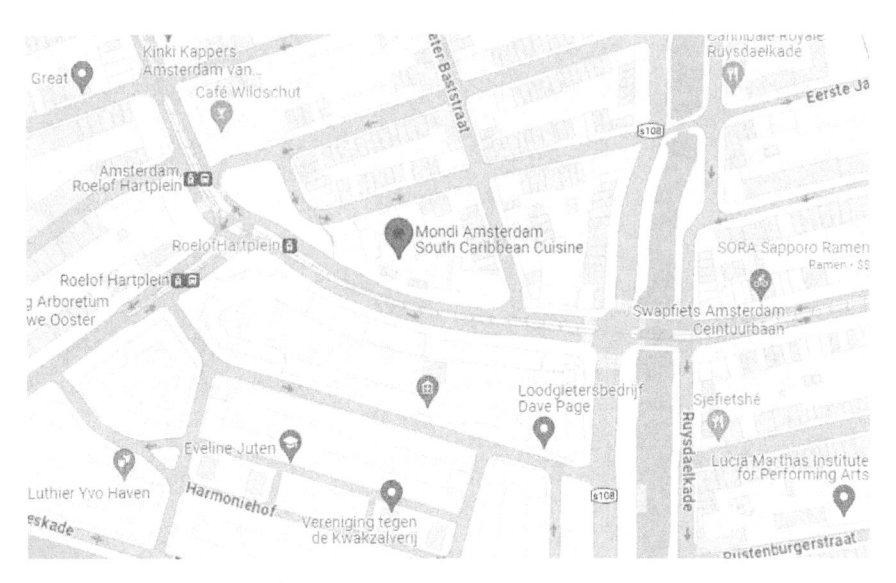

Mondi is the ideal hidden garden, bringing Caribbean delicacies and a welcoming atmosphere to Amsterdam! Mondi provides a communal eating experience with an outdoor terrace and delectable meals. The restaurant's ambiance reflects Caribbean culture and kindness, and you will undoubtedly feel like a very special visitor at Mondi. restaurant.

Address: Roelof Hartstraat 1A

MOON Restaurant

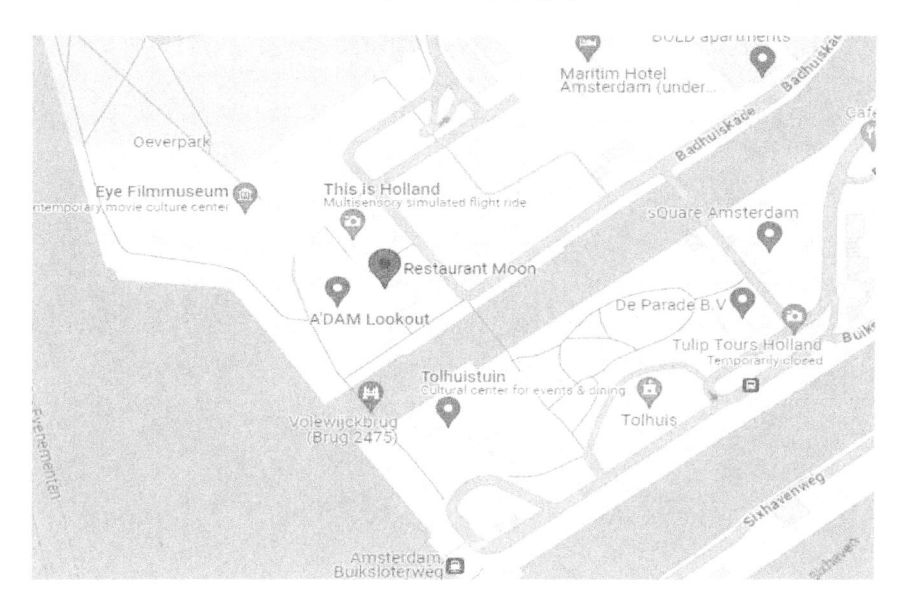

What better way to get to know Amsterdam than to eat dinner overlooking the city? Moon, located on the 19th level of the Amsterdam Tower, is a revolving restaurant that offers a 360-degree view over the picturesque Dutch metropolis. This restaurant provides a wonderful two or three-course dinner experience in a unique setting with courteous service.

Address: Overhoeksplein 3.

Yamazato

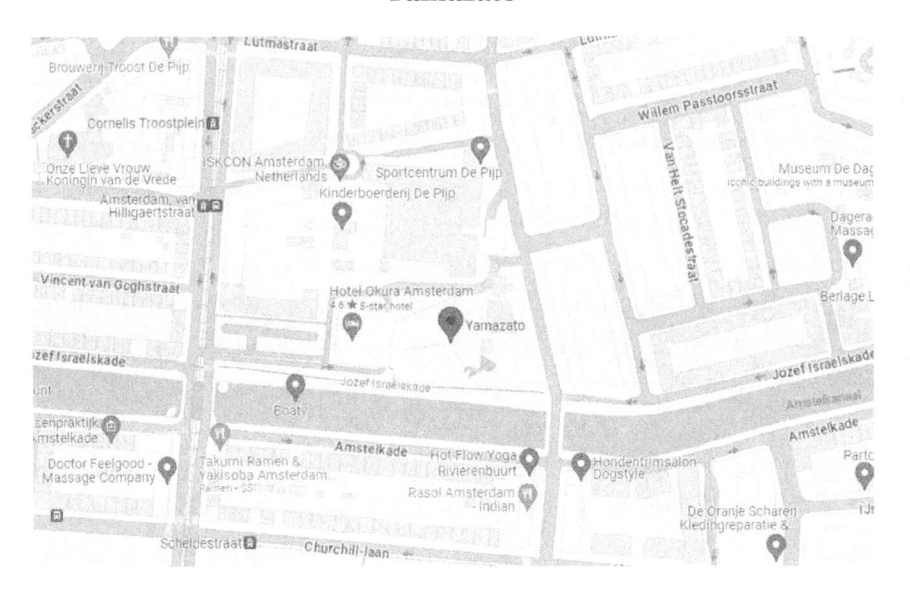

Yamazato, located in the Okura Hotel, has been a Michelin-starred traditional Japanese restaurant since 2002. You'll get to try real Japanese food served by kimono-clad staff.

Yamazato delivers excellent food, including a magnificent 8-course feast that you will not soon forget.

Address: Ferdinand Bolstraat 333.

Meatless District

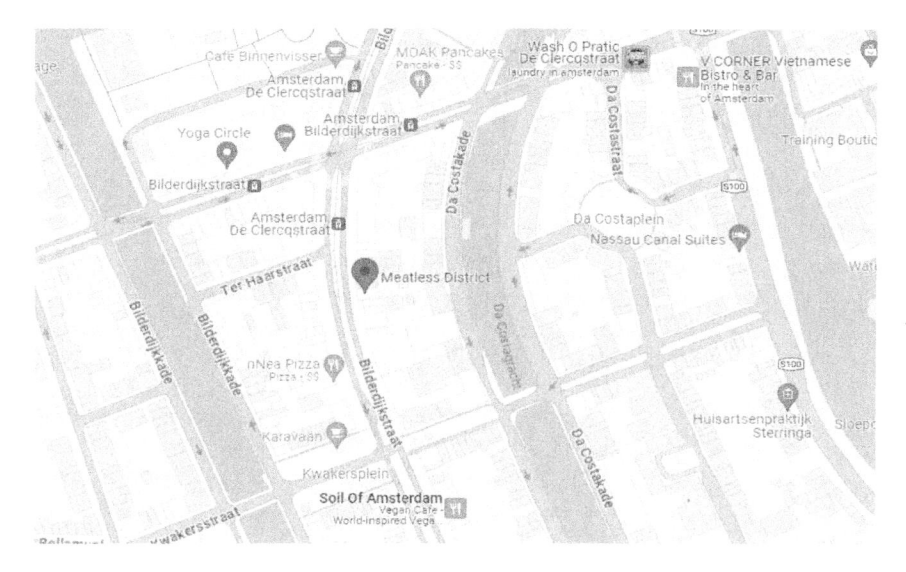

Meatless District is a plant-based restaurant that serves a variety of cuisines produced fresh every day. The restaurant provides high-quality food at moderate prices.

Meatless District serves the finest vegan burger I've ever had! This eatery is a must-visit for all vegetarians. The Meatless District, a colorful and comfortable restaurant with friendly staff, serves a variety of cuisines ranging from soups to salads and burgers.

Address: Bilderdijkstraat 65–67.

De Plantage Restaurant

De Plantage delivers delicious and unusual cuisine from its large terrace in a bright and trendy setting. This restaurant, known for its picturesque setting, is ideal for lunch or dinner.

The emphasis is on the spectacular views and the option to sit comfortably inside or outside while enjoying pleasant service and a mouthful of delicacy.

Address: Plantage Kerklaan 36.

Mr. and Mrs. Watson

Mr. & Mrs. Watson is a plant-based cheesery and restaurant that offers the ultimate vegan experience. If you are a vegan and a cheese lover, this will be your favorite restaurant in the city.

Mr. & Mrs. Watson is a hidden gem with a nice atmosphere, an extensive menu, and a welcoming staff. This restaurant is ideal for a cozy evening of cheese and wine, as well as a pleasant supper.

Address: Linnaeuskade 3H

Vapiano

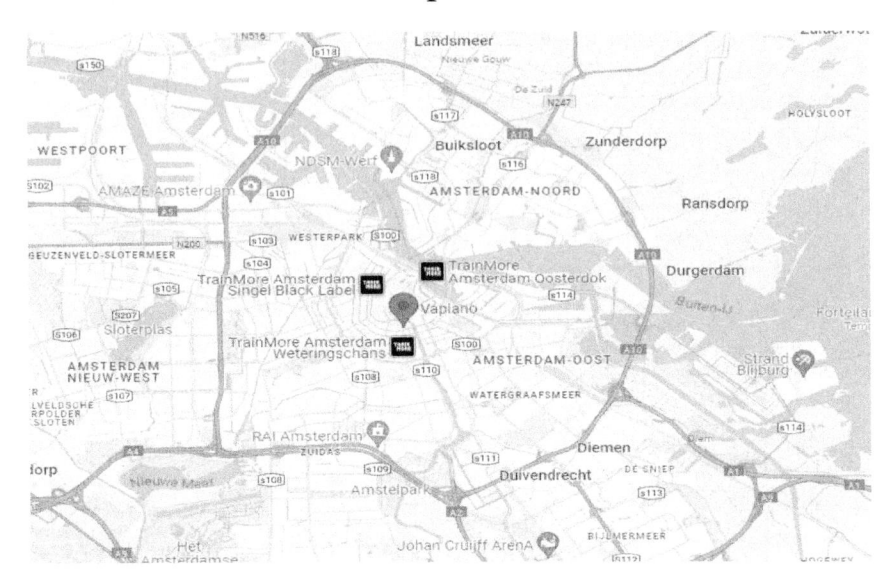

If you're looking for a quick and reasonable supper while seeing the city, this is the place to go. Vapiano is a modern Italian restaurant offering lunch options such as fresh pizza, spaghetti, and salads.

The speed and convenience of ordering at this restaurant may help you unwind after a long day of exploring the city. To get even faster service, call the restaurant ahead of time or order online for pick-up. This is the spot to acquire tasty cuisine quickly.

Address: Amstelstraat 2–4

The Pantry

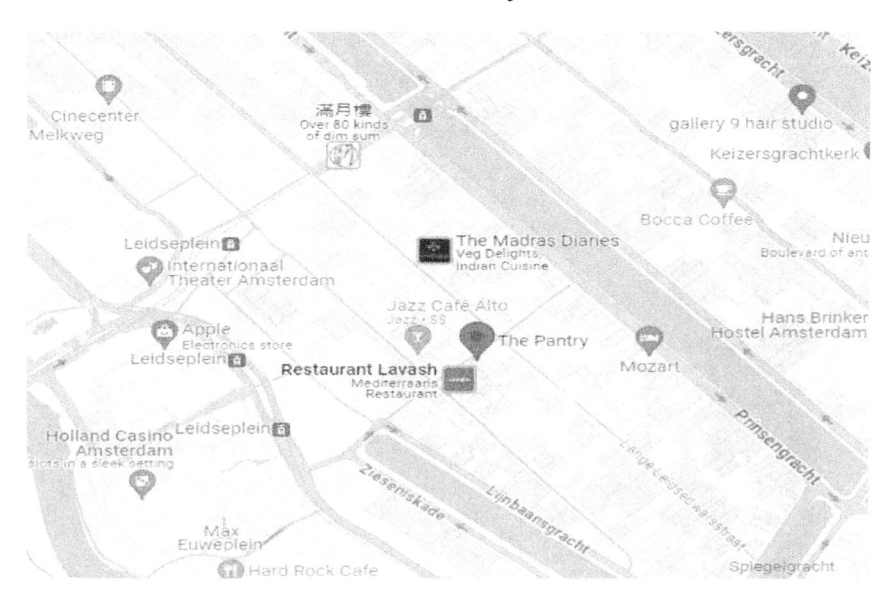

The Pantry is a great and inexpensive spot to experience Dutch cuisine while in Amsterdam. It's the ideal place to have traditional Dutch home-cooked meals. The Pantry is a local favorite in Amsterdam because it delivers high-quality, delicious food.

Address: Leidsekruisstraat 21.

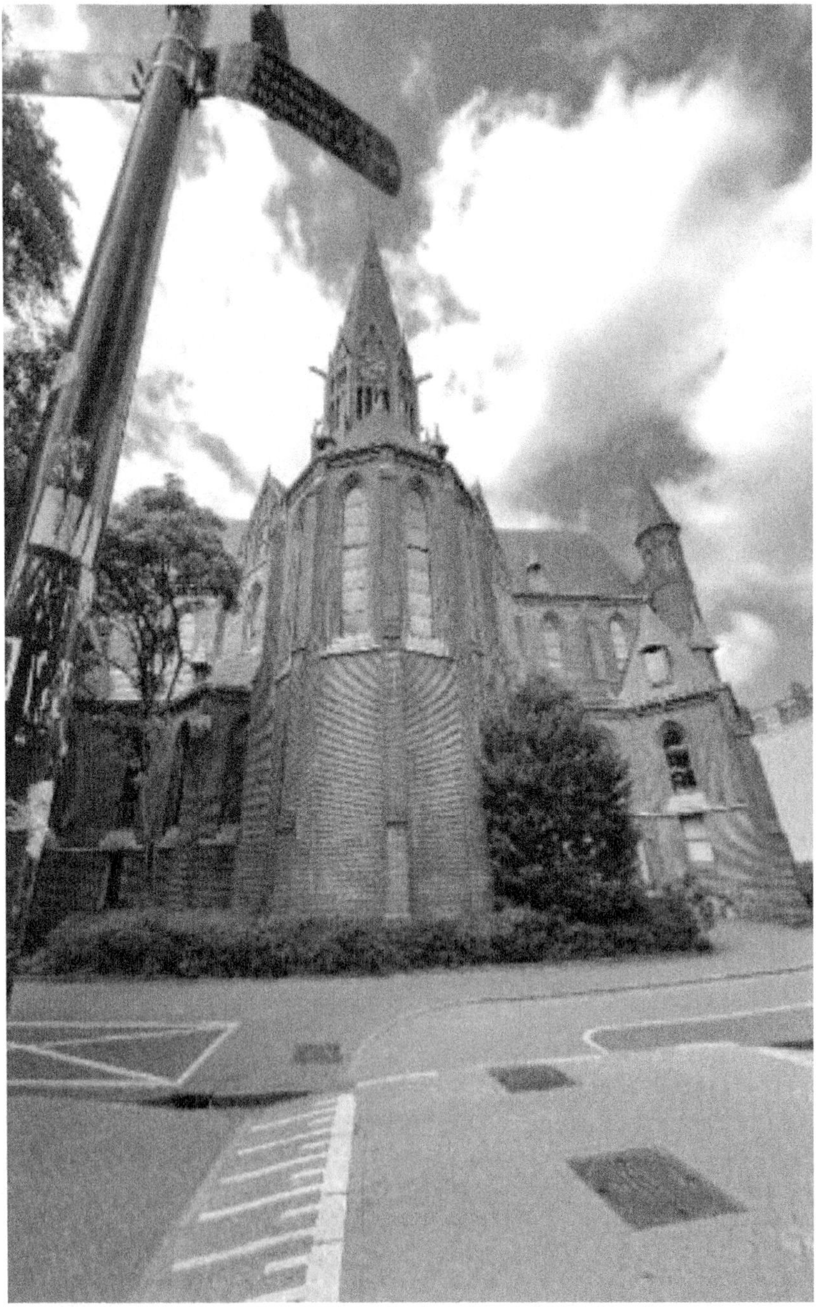

Dutch Cuisine and Culinary Delights

Amsterdam provides the hungry traveler with a variety of interesting gastronomic experiences, ranging from small pancakes to croquettes from a vending machine. Don't leave without sampling at least one of these traditional Dutch dishes.

Bitterballen

So you went out for a few cocktails. You neglected to eat dinner. The 8% Belgian beers are starting to take their toll. What to do? The solution is in the bitterballen. Delicious, deep-fried crispy balls generally served with mustard for dipping - they're the perfect Dutch pub snack and can be found on the menu at most Amsterdam bars.

Stroopwafels

Stroopwafels are a must-try Dutch sweet delight. Two thin waffles sandwiched together with a coating of sugary syrup; these scrumptious treats are best savored hot and gooey from a street market or bakery.

Frietjes

Yes, but not any fries. Trust us. You could see these thick-sliced fries on menus as patat or frites, and they are generally served in a steaming hot paper cone covered with a variety of delectable toppings. Request a 'patatje oorlog' for a dollop of peanut satay sauce, mayo, and onions, or a 'patat special' for a combination of curry ketchup, mayonnaise, and onion.

Pannenkoeken

Unlike the thick and fluffy American pancake, Dutch pannenkoeken (pancakes) have a thinner, crepe-like consistency with more surface area for tasty toppings. Order yours filled with fruit, cream, and syrup from our selections of the top pancake restaurants in Amsterdam.

Jenever

Jenever, the forerunner to gin, is not a food but plays an equally essential part in Dutch gastronomy. This liquor, made from juniper berries, has a malty flavor comparable to whiskey and was originally used for medicinal purposes before becoming one of the country's defining beverages. It's commonly served in a tulip-shaped glass with a beer, a combination known as a kopstootje, which means "head butt".

Appletaart

As if you needed an excuse to have a delicious slice of apple pie. The deep-dish Dutch version is laced with cinnamon, sprinkled with raisins, and served until topped with whipped cream. Though it tops the dessert menu at most restaurants and cafés, Winkel 43 in the Jordaan area, as well as nearby Cafe 't Papeneiland, are regarded to serve one of the best.

Kibbeling

If you're not feeling courageous enough to try raw herring (see above), you can still get your fish fix with kibbeling. They're just as wonderful as they look, and they're usually served with a mayonnaise-based herb sauce and lemon. For the greatest kibbling experience, have it hot and fresh from a street market (we recommend Dappermarkt and Ten Katemarkt).

Kroketten

We're not talking Michelin-standard cuisine here, but these hole-in-the-wall cafés make the list of Dutch must-tries only for their novelty value. Head into any FEBO and you'll find a variety of hot appetizers behind glass doors, including hamburgers, kroketten, and frikandellen. Put some coins in the slot, and the meal is served.

Oliebollen

The name translates to 'oil balls', but don't let that put you off. Essentially, they are deep-fried sweet doughnuts (occasionally with fruit pieces) sprinkled in powdered sugar, and they are so delectable that they are only available around New Year's Eve, shortly before the January diet begins.

Kaas

Visit one of Amsterdam's many 'kaas' stores or markets to sample Gouda, Geitenkaas, or Maasdammer, as cheese is a major industry in the Netherlands. Stop by one of the Henri Willig Cheese and More stores for an introduction to the most famous Dutch cheeses, or visit the Reypenaer Tasting Room for a professionally guided tasting of their award-winning selections.

Poffertjes

Repeat after us. 'PO-fer-jus'. These small fluffy clouds of delicious goodness are available at restaurants, street markets, and pancake houses across Amsterdam, but nothing beats a bag of hot, buttery poffertjes from a street market vendor. Sprinkle them with powdered sugar and let the fun begin.

Ontbijtkoek

This delectable ginger cake comes in loaves and is dense enough that one slice is always sufficient. The name translates to 'morning cake'; however, you can eat it at any time of day because you're an adult and no one will stop you. Spread some thick butter on top for extra yumminess.

Stamppot

Stamppot is the ultimate Dutch comfort meal, similar to British Bubble & Squeak, and ideal for cold winter evenings. Translated precisely as 'mash pot', this traditional cuisine consists of potatoes mashed with additional vegetables, such as sauerkraut, carrot, onion, or kale, and is typically served with a large juicy sausage.

Snert

Snert. You heard us. Holland's pea soup is a thick green stew made with split peas, pork, celery, onions, and leeks that, despite its name, is quite excellent. Snert, a hearty winter snack popular throughout the Netherlands, is usually served by street vendors to ice skaters on the frozen canals.

Coffee Shops vs. Cafés: A Local Experience

Drip-brew coffee, organic micro-roasters, and delectable flat whites: wherever you go in this city, you'll never be far from a superb blend. Read on for a rundown of our favorite coffee shops in town.

Friedhats FUKU Café

Friedhats FUKU Cafe is located in Amsterdam's lively Bos en Lommer sector. Here, you'll find excellently roasted, delicious coffee prepared by award-winning baristas. For this crew, the greatest sustainable coffee comes straight from growers or European distributors. Their lively cafe serves delicious kimchi sandwiches and lemon cakes, as well as various drinks such as specialty beers. But for our money, this is the coffee you should try.

Friedhats FUKU Café at Bos en Lommerweg 136, Bos en Lommer

Back to black

Back to Black has two locations in Amsterdam and serves freshly roasted coffee and baked goodies. Sip a ristretto and treat yourself to one of their freshly baked pastries while relaxing in this pleasant café with a very American throwback vibe. They care deeply about the environment, therefore you'll notice that they use sustainable practices in all they do. They also see their roasted beans, so why not get a bag when you leave?

Van Hallstraat 268, Westerpark; Weteringstraat 48, Spiegelkwartier; Back to Black

Barmhartig

At Barmhartig, you must climb a stairway to reach coffee paradise, but it is well worth the effort. This café overlooks IJhaven in the city's east, providing a great view alongside your caffeine shot. Choose from espresso,

Aeropress, or slow drip, and for something a little less stimulating but equally excellent, try a chai, tea, or freshly squeezed juice.

Barmhartig | Veemkade 1288, Oostende Eilanden

EspressoFabriek

Established in 2005, the EspressoFabriek is regarded as a pioneer of specialty coffee in Amsterdam, having been one of the first enterprises to roast their beans in-house. Not only is their coffee delicious, but the space is stunning, with high ceilings and elegant architectural elements. Grab a coffee to go for a walk in Westerpark, or, if you have kids, give yourself a little boost before spending the rest of the day at the nearby sandpit.

EspressoFabriek | Pazzanistraat 39, Westerpark; Roepie Kruizestraat 2, Zeeburgereiland; IJburglaan 1489, IJburg

30 mL Coffee Roasters

In terms of coffee, 30ml is the amount of espresso used to make a latte, flat white, or cappuccino. 30ml Coffee Roasters, one of Utrecht's most popular coffee shops, is preparing to conquer Amsterdam with its Europaplein branch. Green coffee beans are roasted to perfection, yielding an ideal combination for great filter coffee, latte macchiato, and cortado. As an added benefit, they provide breakfast all day!

Van Noordtstraat 26, Westerpark/Bijlmerplein 156, Zuidoost Coffee Roasters, 30 ml

Lot Sixty One

Lot Sixty-One, run by two Australians who came to Amsterdam via some of New York's most recognized coffee shops, is a small, light café, shop, and roastery on Kinkerstraat. Snag a seat outside, enjoy your excellent cup of coffee in the sun, and don't forget to pick up some fresh beans to take home.

Lot 61 | Kinkerstraat 112, Oud-West.

Coffee Bru

Single-origin coffee and the perfect flat white: inspired by South African coffee bars, Coffee Bru wants to be an extension of its customers' living rooms with its accessible and laid-back atmosphere. A sunny terrace and a children's play area are the frosting on the cake.

Coffee Bru, Beukenplein 14, Oost.

Rum Baba

The famous rum-drenched French pastries, as well as red velvet cake, cinnamon buns, and other sweet delicacies, are on the menu at this quaint, vintage-y place with a vivid blue floor. Yes, the coffee is also rather delicious.

Rum Baba | Pretoriusstraat 33, Oost/Elandsgracht 134, Jordaan.

The Coffee Virus

This coffee shop in Amsterdam Noord caters to creatives and coffee enthusiasts, where freelancers and entrepreneurs brainstorm new ideas while sipping coffee made with a V60-1, an Aeropress, a Chemex, or a Syphon. The walls of The Coffee Virus are covered in art and graphic design.

The Coffee Virus at Overhoeksplein, Noord

Caffènation

Caffènation, in Amsterdam's Schinkel neighborhood, is a cozy spot with 1950s furnishings, cactus, and the aroma of fresh Belgian coffee. The beans are roasted in Antwerp, and the chocolate is handcrafted, as is customary in Belgium.

Caffeination | Warmondstraat 120, Nieuw West

Vascobelo V-Bar

Sometimes it appears that coffee shops and bookstores were meant to be together, and the Flemish café Vascobelo, located on the first floor above the Scheltema bookstore, is a prime example of this wonderful union. Pour over your recently purchased print products while sipping on a 92-degree Celsius ristretto, a nude doppio, or, if you're feeling extra special, a syrup-infused latte. The old-school mood is completed by photography on the walls and jazz from the speakers.

Vascobelo Scheltema | Rokin 9–15, Royal Mile

De Koffieschenkerij

De Koffieschenkerij, located in Amsterdam's oldest and most infamous Red Light district, is the ideal spot to escape the noise and bustle of this vibrant neighborhood. The former sacristy of their previous church location serves good coffee, traditional sweets, and nutritious lunch alternatives. They focus on organic products, high-quality coffee, and sustainable plantation farming methods.

Oudekerksplein 27, De Koffieschenkerij, The Red Light District (de Wallen)

White Label Coffee/Schuurmanoomkensgrassotti

This specialist roastery has two locations: one on the lively Jan Evertsenstraat in De Baarsjes and one in Noord, where caffeine-loving customers will be delighted with their delicious flat whites and fashionable bags of fresh beans to take home and brew. They also supply

Schuurmanoomkensgrassotti, (we know it's a mouthful to say), a sleek new coffee shop on the Overtoom in Oud-West.

White Label Coffee | Jan Evertsenstraat 13, De Baarsjes/Zonneplein 4, Noord.

Schuurmanoomkensgrassotti - Overtoom 558, Oud-West

Koffie ende Koeck

Koffie ende Koeck's cuisine is fully plant-based, therefore vegans and lactose-intolerant diners can rejoice. Their menu includes vegan pecan pie, petit fours, scuffins (a scone-muffin hybrid), cakes, cookies, and chocolates. Grab a latte made with soy, almond, spelled, or hazelnut milk and a delicious treat. Furthermore, the café's decor has repurposed furniture and fittings.

Koffie en Koeck, Haarlemmerweg 175, Westerpark

Koffie Academie

Koffie Academie's warm atmosphere and central position just around the corner from Vondelpark make it a great place for catching up with friends or getting some work done on a rainy day. Choose from freshly cooked sandwiches, croissants, brownies, or carrot cake, as well as freshly roasted coffee. Sparsely equipped with hefty oak tables and dark walls, the window counter is excellent for watching the world go by, or when enjoying a lonely cup of coffee.

Koffie Academie | Overtoom 95, Oud-West/Radarweg 230, Sloterdijk

Nightlife and Entertainment

Prepare to paint the town red, because Amsterdam is about to give you the fun of your life! In this exciting 2024 edition, we'll take you on a whirlwind tour of the city's biggest parties, complete with glitz, glamour, and pulse-pounding sounds.

From throbbing underground clubs to stylish rooftop soirées, Amsterdam's bustling nightlife provides a playground for those looking for exceptional experiences. We've handpicked the best party places, where electrifying energy, world-class DJs, and one-of-a-kind experiences come together. So put on your dance shoes and get ready to immerse yourself in the seductive beat of the Dutch city. Let's disco until dawn and make memories that will last a lifetime!

Escape

Experience the unequaled nightlife dream at Escape Amsterdam, a legendary nightclub in the center of the city. Escape's exciting atmosphere and throbbing sounds urge partygoers to leave their inhibitions at the door and enjoy a mind-blowing night. Located at Rembrandtplein 11, it is easily accessible to both locals and tourists looking for a memorable experience. Inside, the intensity is evident as colorful lights flood the dancefloor, directing bodies into a mesmerizing dance of oneness. Renowned DJs curate a diverse music selection, ranging from house to techno, hip-hop to R&B. Escape Amsterdam is a place where fantasies come true, allowing you to succumb to an enthralling voyage of pure ecstasy.

Date: Sun, Monday, Tuesday, Wednesday, Thursday, Friday, and Saturday.

Location: Rembrandtplein 11, 1017 CT Amsterdam.

Music: hits

ClubNl

Welcome to ClubNl, Amsterdam's best nightlife! Prepare for an incredible night of nonstop partying and exciting music. ClubNl, located in Nieuwezijds Voorburgwal 169, is the ideal place for people looking for an unforgettable nightlife experience.

ClubNl's vibrant atmosphere will grab you from the moment you walk in. The club has a sleek and modern appearance, complete with cutting-edge lighting and an amazing sound system that will make your heart race with every beat. The dance floor is amply sized, so you can let loose and dance the night away.

When it comes to music, ClubNl ensures an eclectic blend that appeals to all tastes. Whether you prefer house, techno, or R&B, the experienced DJs will keep the energy high all night. Every track performed, from the current hits to underground classics, will have you moving and grooving.

The ClubNl crowd is vibrant and diverse. Expect a mix of locals and foreign partygoers, all united by a passion for music and an amazing experience. Whether you're a seasoned clubber or fresh to the scene, you'll be cordially welcomed. The courteous personnel and pleasant ambiance create an inclusive and vibrant atmosphere, ensuring a memorable night.

If you want to spend an evening with pulsating beats and memories that will last a lifetime, ClubNl is the place to go. So put on your dancing shoes and join us at ClubNl for an event that will leave you wanting more.

Date: Thursday, Friday, Saturday.

Location: Nieuwezijds Voorburgwal 169, 1012 RK Amsterdam.

Music: hits

Twenty-third Bar

Twenty Third Bar, located on Ferdinand Bolstraat, provides a spectacular rooftop experience in Amsterdam. With spectacular city views, perfectly prepared cocktails, and a carefully curated range of excellent wines, this stylish setting is ideal for relaxing with friends or a special someone. The clean, modern decor and comfy seating provide a calm yet polished atmosphere, while carefully chosen music sets the tone for a memorable evening. Whether you're a local or a visitor, Twenty Third Bar guarantees a warm welcome and an unforgettable experience that will boost your night out in the center of the city.

Date: Sun, Monday, Tuesday, Wednesday, Thursday, Friday, and Saturday.

Location: Ferdinand Bolstraat 333, 1072 LH Amsterdam.

Music: hits

W. Lounge

W Lounge, located atop the W Hotel in the heart of Amsterdam, provides a unique rooftop experience with stunning panoramic views of the city skyline. By day, the sleek and contemporary decor provides the ideal setting for a classy getaway. As night sets, the lounge morphs into a dynamic hotspot, with prominent DJs providing a lively environment. The sophisticated audience, which includes both locals and foreign jet-setters, congregates in one of the city's most exclusive locations. Enjoy freshly made beverages and delectable meals from the menu while admiring the breathtaking sunset over the old city below. Whether it's a trendy pre-party place or a sumptuous night out, W Lounge is the best destination for individuals with refined tastes. An evening here guarantees to be unforgettable, with its sophisticated ambiance, exciting music, and stunning vistas.

Date: Sun, Monday, Tuesday, Wednesday, Thursday, Friday, and Saturday.

Location: W Hotel: Spuistraat 175, 1012 VN Amsterdam.

Music: hits

Mondi Sky Bar

Experience the magnificent Mondi SkyBar in the center of Amsterdam, high above the streets. With its sophisticated and opulent atmosphere, this private rooftop bar provides breathtaking panoramic views and chic, comfy seats for a wonderful evening. As the sun sets, the pub transforms into a lively hotspot, complete with pounding sounds and a mixed mixture of locals and international visitors. Indulge in handmade cocktails and delectable tapas while living the high life. Whether you're celebrating a special event or just relaxing, at Mondi SkyBar, where the sky is the limit, you may enhance your evening and have an amazing experience that will have you coming back for more.

Date: Sun, Monday, Tuesday, Wednesday, Thursday, Friday, and Saturday.

Location: Schipholweg 275, 1171 PK Amsterdam.

Music: hits

Jimmy Woo

Jimmy Woo, located in the center of Amsterdam, is a legendary nightclub that flawlessly blends the fascination of the East with the dynamic energy of the city's nightlife. Its elegant ambiance and sumptuous furnishings provide a sense of mystery and seduction, ideal for indulging and escaping. Renowned DJs play a wide mix of house, hip-hop, and R&B, keeping the dance floor alive with pounding sounds. This iconic venue draws a mixed crowd of trendsetters, fashionistas, and socialites, creating an exciting and expectant atmosphere. Jimmy Woo creates an unforgettable experience that keeps guests intrigued and wanting more.

Date: Thursday, Friday, Saturday.

Location: Korte Leidsedwarsstraat 18, 1017 Rc Amsterdam

Music: hits

Air Amsterdam

Experience the pinnacle of Amsterdam's nightlife at AIR Amsterdam, a partying location that improves the experience. Located at Amstelstraat 24, this legendary club attracts the city's elite, providing them with a memorable night of dancing and excitement. As you enter AIR Amsterdam, you'll be transported to a world where music reigns supreme.

The dynamic atmosphere charges every moment, backed by a sophisticated interior design that sets the stage for a memorable night. With a cutting-edge sound system, you can expect heart-stopping beats that will keep you entertained all night long. AIR Amsterdam, known for its eclectic programming, features world-class DJs and cutting-edge musicians from the electronic music industry, ensuring a captivating experience for all music fans. The crowd is similarly amazing, with a mix of local and foreign partygoers united by their love of music. AIR Amsterdam offers an inclusive and lively workplace that values diversity and makes everyone feel welcome. Join the city's nightlife elite and experience a memorable night at AIR Amsterdam, a legendary club that delivers pure entertainment and leaves you wanting more.

Date: Sun, Thursday, Friday, Saturday.

Location: Amstelstraat 24, 1017 DA Amsterdam.

Music: hits

LuminAir

LuminAir Amsterdam is a magnificent rooftop hideaway that provides breathtaking views of the city skyline. Located in Oosterdoksstraat 4, Level 11, this trendy and modern facility has an attractive and sophisticated ambiance, ideal for a memorable day or night out. As the sun goes down, the atmosphere comes alive with vivid beats and electric energy, attracting a diverse crowd of locals and international tourists. From lunchtime cocktails to late-night partying, LuminAir is the best venue for anyone wishing to enjoy Amsterdam's nightlife while admiring the stunning views. It's the place to go if you want a truly remarkable and luxurious experience.

Date: Sun, Monday, Tuesday, Wednesday, Thursday, Friday, and Saturday.

Location: Oosterdokstraat 4, Level 11, 1011 DK Amsterdam.

Music: hits

Club Prime

Club Prime Amsterdam is a sophisticated and thrilling nightclub on Rembrandtplein 22, in the heart of Amsterdam. Upon entering, guests are met with a lively atmosphere packed with pulsating sounds and a varied choice of music genres curated by top-tier DJs. The club draws a multicultural population that combines locals and tourists, resulting in a lively and diverse ambiance. What distinguishes Club Prime is its dedication to creating an exclusive and extravagant experience, complete with precisely designed decor, outstanding service, and sumptuous VIP areas that offer premium bottle service. Join us at Club Prime for an extraordinary night of dancing, breathtaking visuals, and fantastic music.

Date: Sun, Monday, Tuesday, Wednesday, Thursday, Friday, and Saturday.

Location: Rembrandtplein 22, 1017 CV Amsterdam.

Music: hits

Experience Amsterdam's bustling and exhilarating nightlife like never before! Our selected list of the Top 10+ Parties in Amsterdam is your ticket to remarkable experiences in the Dutch capital. This list includes anything from cutting-edge electronic music to popular martini clubs.

Dance the night away at iconic clubs like De School, immerse yourself in the unique atmosphere of Supperclub, or attend spectacular rooftop parties at A'DAM Tower. Whether you're a seasoned partygoer or just seeking a taste of Amsterdam's vibrant environment, our carefully chosen locations will provide an unforgettable experience.

Unleash your inner party animal and immerse yourself in the vibrant energy of Amsterdam's party scene. Prepare to make lifelong memories as you immerse yourself in the never-ending excitement and unsurpassed elegance that this captivating city has to offer.

Month by Month Festivals and Events

A new year in Amsterdam brings fresh chances and activities that will keep you occupied and excited. There's much to do in the capital, from traditional holidays like Queer & Pride and King's Day to food and wine festivals, art exhibitions, and amazing theatrical productions. Check out this year's Cultural Agenda to remain informed about what the city has to offer.

January

January is a traditionally dreary month for many, but Amsterdam's coziness makes it a little more palatable than others. New Year's Day (1 January) is a restorative day, with walks, shopping, and perhaps a cold but revitalizing dip to enjoy. It's a terrific month to visit some of Amsterdam's coziest neighborhood pubs, such as those in cozy De Pijp, or attend one of the many candlelight concerts held throughout the winter. The third Saturday of January (19 January) is National Tulip Day, and you can select your tulips from a flower field on Dam Square. If you still want to brave the cold, this is your final chance to see the dazzling lights of the Amsterdam Light Festival, which continues through January 21.

The best month for Frosty boat rides and cruises on the city's peaceful waterways.

February

One of the most difficult aspects of February is that it feels like January all over again, but fortunately, Amsterdam has a plethora of activities to keep you entertained throughout the month. The Lunar New Year begins on February 10, which is an excellent opportunity to visit ancient Nieuwmarkt and Zeedijk while also savoring some of the city's greatest dim sum eateries. Romance descends on February 14th, but much of what makes

Amsterdam so romantic may be experienced alone, with friends, or with partners. Visit one of the city's most atmospheric restaurants, take a stroll around the canals, or attend classical music at the Concertgebouw or Bimhuis. While you're in Amsterdam, don't miss out on Pancake Day (February 21).

The best month to escape to the riverside town of Weesp.

March

As our culture guide to spring demonstrates, the early days of spring are among the greatest the city has to offer. Ramadan begins on March 10, and it's worth exploring Amsterdam's options for iftar. The National Holocaust Museum, which opens in March, is expected to be a moving and significant stop for museum visitors. St Patrick's Day (17 March) occurs just before the flower season begins, making it an ideal time to visit Amsterdam's greatest Irish bars. The main event in March, however, is the opening of the Keukenhof (21 March), a large park of tulips and daffodils best explored on foot. It also marks the start of the cherry blossom season in Amsterdamsebos. And what better way to honor the end of March than with something equally associated with Amsterdam: techno. DGTL (29-31 March) is an environmentally sound dance music festival including strong hitters from the underground electronica scene.

Best month to explore the flower-filled places in and around the city.

April

With spring in the air, most people are upbeat, and it's not just because of the free-flowing caffeine at The Amsterdam Coffee Festival (4-6 April), which brings together the capital's greatest roasters. It's the weather and everything going on, such as the Kaboom Animation Festival (5 April) and the Tulp Festival (10 years), which blooms over the capital in April. The

Amsterdam Wine Festival (18-21 April) opens the cases for a four-day fruity event, just in time for King's Day, a major, country-wide celebration of the reigning monarch, on April 27th.

The best month for Wandering through Amsterdam's bustling city center, naturally dressed in orange.

May

May is one of the best months for weather in Amsterdam, so take advantage of it by celebrating in the city's parks. Liberation Day (5 May) commemorates the Netherlands' liberation from German rule, and the city celebrates with a variety of performances and activities spanning Dam Square to the Jewish Quarter and beyond. Art on Paper takes place on May 9, while Rolling Kitchens (15-19 May) is a food truck festival that transforms a portion of Westerpark into an enormous open-air restaurant. Speaking of the West, 24H West has arrived, which means that for one day in May, the capital's westerly area will be alive with events that encapsulate what it represents. The month concludes with Amsterdam Art Week (29 May-2 June).

The best month to tour the cobblestone alleys and canal-cut towns of Old Holland.

June

Summer has arrived, allowing Amsterdam to finally enjoy its alfresco side, and the cultural agenda focuses on the outdoors. Taste of Amsterdam. June marks the start of festival season in the Netherlands and Amsterdam, with music at the Vondel Park Open Air Festival, rooftop screenings at the On the Roof Film Festival, and a little bit of everything at the Holland Festival, all of which begin and run throughout the month, and in some cases, the entire summer. Taste of Amsterdam serves up its yearly variety of culinary morsels, kicking off the summer food festival season (1 June), while the Bacchus Wine Festival runs for two weeks (7-9 June, 14-16 June), and the Red Light Jazz Festival (8-11 June) commemorates Amsterdam's jazz tradition. While you're outside, you might as well enjoy some of Amsterdam's green spaces: Open Garden Days begins, allowing tourists to explore the city's gorgeous canal gardens.

Best month for: Exploring the region's history through castles and gardens.

July

The middle of summer may see Amsterdam residents fly for warmer shores, but the schedule of activities in the city's parks entices many to stay and even more to visit. Keti Koti takes place on July 1st, a day when the capital honors the abolition of slavery in Suriname and the Antilles. Plenty is going on, both instructive and celebratory, in and around Amsterdam's oldest park, Oosterpark. Elsewhere, the modern dance event Julidans takes center stage, promising orchestrated magic, while Kwaku in Zuidoost adds multicultural flavor to Nelson Mandela Park. July concludes on a high note with Milkshake, a weekend-long festival (26-28 July) for the open-minded and daring to express themselves.

The best month for Visiting pioneering Oostvaardersplassen in New Land.

August

The end of summer is a bright occasion on all fronts. August is in full swing thanks to Queer & Pride (27 July-4 August), which generously paints the canals and their residences in rainbow colors for the Canal Parade (3 August). It's a two-week celebration of Amsterdam's rich variety. Techno fans may look forward to Dekmantel in lush Amsterdamse Bos (5-7

August), while classic and jazz fans can enjoy the Grachtenfestival (9-18 August), which has orchestras and musicians performing along Amsterdam's canals. If film is your favored medium, you're in luck: H'ART Museum opens its open-air theater in August, and the Bijlmerbios film festival takes place in Zuidoost. Finally, Mysteryland (30 August-1 September) combines fairy tales and technology.

The best month for Outdoor cinema rendezvous on rooftops and along canals.

September

Autumn's cold but often sunny skies set in action the gradual transition from outside to indoor cultural activities. The Dutch Theatre Festival (5-15 September) features a variety of spectacular plays, while the Amsterdam Fringe Festival welcomes the avant-garde, and Open Monuments Day (7-8 September) allows visitors to see the city's many architectural masterpieces. Before the weather cools down, some Amsterdam residents participate in the City Swim to raise funds for an ALS charity, or they register for the Dam tot Damloop, a 16-kilometer run from Amsterdam to Zaandam. If the weather is still too cold for you, immerse yourself in the narrative at Read My World or explore pioneering photography at Unseen Amsterdam (19-22 September).

The best month for Exploring Oost's wide cultural agenda during 24-Hour Oost.

October

In October, the Netherlands celebrates Black Achievement Month with concerts, exhibitions, and more. To get started, visit the Black Archives. Another huge event in October is the Amsterdam Dance Event (ADE), which takes place over five days (16-20 October) and features lectures, workshops, discussions, and, of course, parties centered around dance and electronic music. Elsewhere, runners not at ADE (or those with real stamina) prepare for the Amsterdam Marathon (20 October), while the Cinekid film festival (22-25 October) is geared at children, with interactive exhibitions, games, and even the opportunity to meet directors. End the month with a journey to the forest-covered Amstelveen to celebrate Diwali, the Hindu festival of lights.

Best month for dipping your toes into Amsterdam's booming electronic music scene.

November

Even while everyone retreats indoors, Amsterdam's cultural agenda never stops. The International Storytelling Festival Amsterdam takes place in late October and early November, with many activities held in English, while Museumnaacht (4 November) brings the city's cultural institutions to life with unique programming that runs late into the night. For those who celebrate, Sinterklaas appears on November 18 to spread holiday cheer. Though available to anyone, you might find the more serious-inclined tourist and resident at the International Documentary Film Festival (IDFA), which runs from November 13 to 24 and presents a jam-packed schedule of some of the world's most harrowing documentaries.

Best month for: Taking a boat over to ever-fashionable Amsterdam-Noord

December

As the winter darkness settles, Amsterdam practically lights up. The Amsterdam Light Festival (1 December–20 January) is the capital's yearly exile of the shadow, with a changing theme tied to the light works that cling to the canals and the city's numerous crooked corners during December and most of January. Christmas fever has set town, bringing with it Christmas markets, The Amsterdam Winter Paradise (14-30 December), and plenty of ice skating chances. When New Year's (December 31) arrives, make sure to get a good view of the city's (electric) fireworks display, or save room for a night and day of partying in classic Amsterdam style.

Best month for: A cheerful day excursion to charming Haarlem.

And that concludes the year; we'll see you in the next, which promises to be just as excellent, if not better, than the previous one.

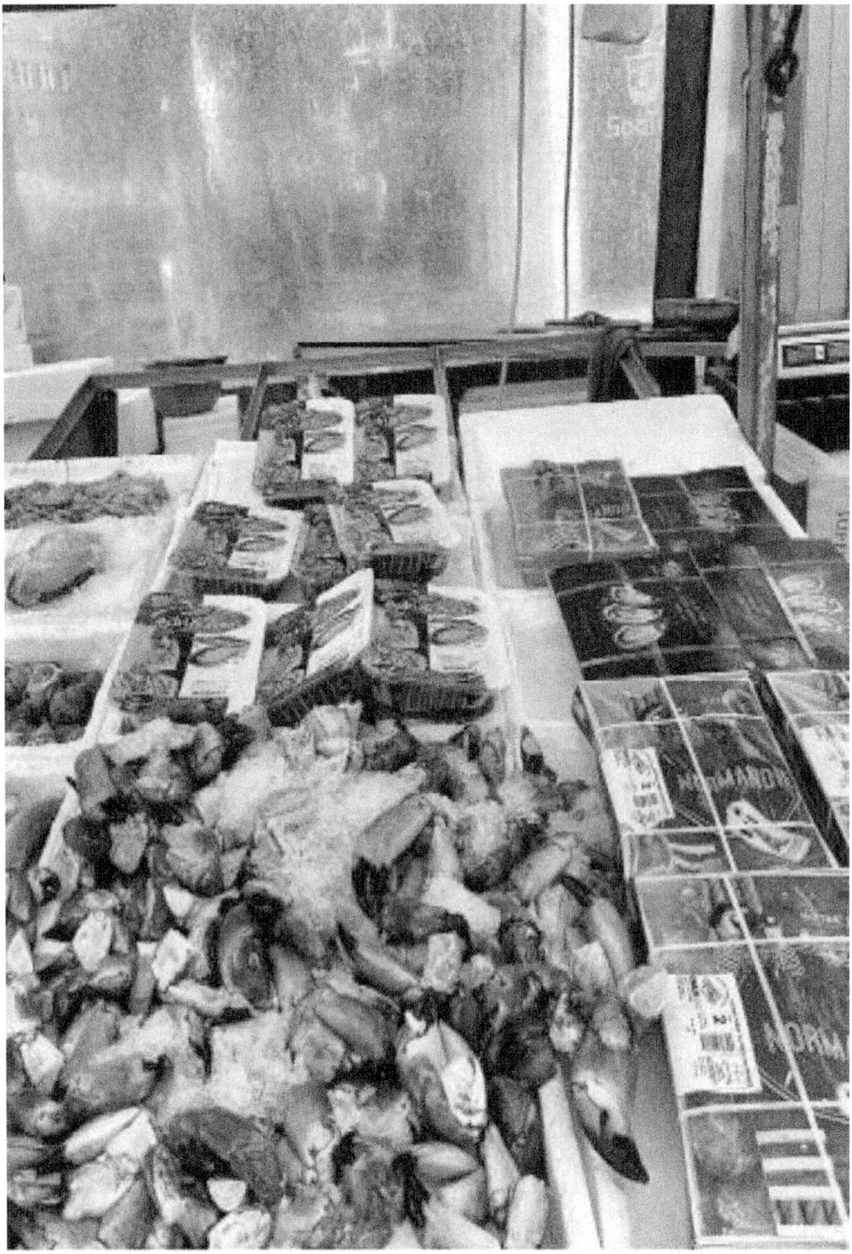

Shopping in Amsterdam

No matter what you're looking for, Amsterdam is a shopping wonderland. For those with more discerning tastes, the city features an outstanding assortment of luxury shops, ranging from designer fashion houses to unique boutiques and custom-made things that cannot be found elsewhere.

Luxury Shopping Streets in Amsterdam

The beautiful neighborhoods you'll find along the way add to the allure of Amsterdam's unique shopping experience. While there are a few high-end department stores in the center, you'll sometimes have to walk past the tourist destinations to find fantastic businesses buried away amongst more residential lanes.

P. C. Hooftstraat

Since the 1970s, the P.C. Hooftstraat, named after the 17th-century poet and dramatist Pieter Corneliszoon Hooft, has served as an upmarket retail destination. Located near the Museumplein, this street is your first visit for big-name labels like Hugo Boss, D&G, MaxMara, Ralph Lauren, Hermes, Gucci, and more, as well as high-end jewelers like Boutique Tourbillon.

De Bijenkorf

On the outskirts of Dam Square, de Bijenkorf will keep you engaged for hours. The assortment includes everything from apparel, purses, and shoes to housewares, luggage, and electronics. On the ground floor, there are various luxury shop-in-shops, including Louis Vuitton, Hermes, and Gucci.

Van Baerlestraat

Van Baerlestraat, just around the corner from P.C. Hooftstraat, is home to several well-known Dutch fashion designers such as Pauw, The People of the Labyrinths, and Fred de la Bretonière, who are noted for their useful yet attractive boots and handbags. Rivet Ledertassen also carries a nice assortment of (designer) leather purses. If you want to be pampered, make an appointment at the Soap Treatment Store for a facial, manicure, or massage.

Willemsparkweg

Continue on the magnificent Willemsparkweg from the Van Baerlestraat into Amsterdam Zuid. Oog in Oog sells designer (sun)glasses, and Thalian has an excellent outfit selection. Edha Interieur is a must-visit for those who appreciate unique furniture and lighting. If you want to get a bite and rest your feet, the Willemsparkweg provides a selection of appealing cafés and eateries to choose from.

Cornelis Schuytstraat

Halfway along the Willemsparkweg, you'll cross the Cornelis Schuytstraat, which is ideal for putting together an entirely new outfit. Step into French Connection for the best of British design. Admire luxury shoes at Shoebaloo or Manwood, then visit one of the street's many jewelers to locate the ideal earrings or watch.

Beethovenstraat

The Beethovenstraat, located a few blocks from the Cornelis Schuytstraat, is a relatively small shopping street with numerous hidden treasures. Popular Dutch designers like Pauw and Claudia Sträter may be found here, along with jewelers and specialty boutiques. Sterre & Tijl sells beautiful baby furniture, toys, and clothing, while The English Hatter sells hats for the elegant gentleman. If your desire for luxury extends to cuisine, visit Huize van Wely for incredible chocolate bonbons or Tromp for exquisite cheeses.

All that glitters...

Amsterdam, one of Europe's diamond capitals, is the best destination to shop for jewelry. You can purchase loose diamonds here, however you may prefer jewelry that can be worn outside the store. Visit Gassan or Coster Diamonds for insider information on the diamond industry, as well as the option to shop. There are some tiny specialty jewelers on the retail streets listed above, but famous brands like Bvlgari, Cartier, and Tiffany & Co, travel straight to P.C. Hooftstraat.

Conservatorium Hotel (Van Baerle Gallery)

Wander through this glittering shopping gallery to get a taste of Dutch style and ultra-exclusive brands. Bonebakker sells jewelry, Club Cinq sells children's apparel and bedding, and La Casa del Habano has the Netherlands' greatest collection of Cuban cigars.

Explore Out and about in the Amsterdam Metropolitan Area

There's more to the Amsterdam Metropolitan Area than picturesque polders, cheese, and windmills. Visit the waterfront in Lelystad and indulge in some luxury shopping at Batavia Stad. It may appear to be a quaint village, but it is an outlet shopping center with hundreds of big-name brands at affordable costs.

Fashion

Floris Van Bommel

Floris van Bommel has you covered with moccasins, loafers, sneakers, and brogues. Discover the renowned men's brand 'Van Bommel' at its Singel and Van Baerlestraat locations.

Tenue de Nimes

The denim experts at Tenue de Nimes can help you select the best-fitting jeans. Enjoy a fresh coffee or craft beer while perusing a variety of denim labels from across the world, and take advantage of complimentary changes.

Amélie Guépin

Tailor-made clothing is unquestionably the pinnacle of luxury, and if you want to look and feel your best for a special occasion, Dutch couturier Amelie Guepin can assist you in creating a one-of-a-kind garment that is tailored to you.

Salon Heleen Huisman

Salon Heleen Huisman is a great place to find a second-hand designer gem, from Balenciaga to Prada and Loewe, while also supporting sustainability. The showroom in Jacob Obrechtstraat, near Vondelpark, is exclusively open by appointment.

Love Stories

If you agree with Love Stories' idea - "lingerie is part of your outfit - the first layer, your mood for the day" - include this Amsterdam-based boutique in your shopping trip.

Ace&Tate offers the most recent trends in glasses and sunglasses, while Afura and Filling Pieces offer more high-end fashion.

Jewellery

Gassan

Gassan, a family-owned business, has 75 years of diamond industry experience and can guide consumers on how to confidently select a cut. Looking for something with a little more weight? The jeweler is also an authorized dealer for over 20 of the world's most prominent jewelry brands and over 60 premium watch brands.

Coster

Royal Coster Diamonds, founded in 1840, is the world's oldest diamond polishing facility, and its clients include several European royals. The store, which sells polished diamonds and exquisite diamond jewelry, also wants to educate visitors about Amsterdam's sparkling legacy through workshop tours.

Beauty

Skin and Cosmetics

Skins Cosmetics has world-renowned brands like Diptyque, Aesop, Creed, and Laura Mercier, so you can find the perfect skincare treatment, perfume, or make-up. Fully qualified staff are there to provide personalized guidance, and a make-up artist is ready to give you that much-needed touch-up from shopping to dinner.

Furniture and Lifestyle

Saltwater

Salt Water's simple yet exquisite kitchenware and decor line at Haarlemmerdijk draws inspiration from Malaysian heritage, California beaches, and the laid-back Australian lifestyle. It mixes artisanship, wabi-sabi aesthetics, and natural living.

The GatherShop

The Gathershop, which supports tiny design studios and individual creators, has joined a few concept stores at De Hallen.

Mendo

This store, known as the "home of aesthetically pleasing books," is where you may discover the perfect book to brighten up your bookshelf or coffee table. Mendo's main store at Hotel De L'Europe features rows of books on fashion, architecture, travel, and food, as well as a special selection of collector's editions. The area is visually appealing, with soft lighting and muted tones that make guests feel at ease and inspired.

Food

Puccini Bombini

No sugar, butter, fondant, or artificial additions. Instead, there's plenty of chocolate and surprising ingredients like pepper, rhubarb, tea, and calvados. Here's how Puccini produces chocolate. Find your favourite flavour on Staalstraat or Singel 184.

Pompadour

After a day of shopping on the Nine Streets, stop by Pompadour and be transported to a French tearoom. Enjoy bonbons, cakes, and other delectable delicacies.

Tax-free shopping

Remember that non-EU residents can claim the VAT back on purchases made in the European Union. In the Netherlands, VAT is 21%, and the minimum purchase is €50. To get a refund, visit Customs before leaving the EU and obtain a stamp. You can either return the stamped receipt to the retailer for a complete VAT refund or use the following services:

Only shop at Global Blue-affiliated retailers. Request a tax-free cheque, and then reclaim the VAT at the airport desk. For additional information, please visit www.global-blue.com.

Shop wherever you like, keep your purchase receipt, and then recover the VAT online or at the VAT Free service desk in Amsterdam Airport Schiphol, departure hall 3. Visit www.vatfree.com for additional information.

Cultural Etiquette and Local Customs

The Function of the Family

- The Dutch regard the family as the cornerstone of the social order.
- Families are often small, consisting of one or two children.
- In comparison to many other countries, few women work outside the home full-time.
- This helps women to be more present with their children throughout the day.

Dutch manners

- Appearance is important to the Dutch.
- They are disciplined, cautious, and detail-oriented.
- They consider themselves economical, diligent, practical, and well-organized.
- They put a high priority on cleanliness and neatness.
- At the same time, the Dutch are extremely private people.
- They do not call attention to themselves and do not place a great value on the trappings of success that other Western societies do.
- They abhor shows of riches because they contradict their egalitarian principles.
- They do not boast about their achievements or material goods.

Egalitarianism

- The Dutch are egalitarian and quite accepting of individual variations.
- Their children are raised free of gender preconceptions.

- The country has almost no abject poverty due to social programs, which, nevertheless, increase the tax burden on labor.
- This egalitarian perspective is carried over to the workplace.
- Even in hierarchical organizations, everyone has the right to express their opinions and have them heard.
- The manager may be the final decision-maker, but he or she will normally seek input from employees and aim for consensus.
- Everyone is cherished and respected.

Dutch Privacy

- When it comes to dealing with strangers, the Dutch are reserved and formal.
- They are private individuals who do not publicly display their things or emotions.
- Self-control is thought to be a virtue.
- The Dutch do not ask personal inquiries, and if you trespass on their privacy, they will refuse to answer.
- Personal lives are kept separate from business.
- If a friendship forms at work and spreads to the personal sphere, this camaraderie will not be transferred into the workplace.
- Personal concerns are not addressed with friends, regardless of their closeness.

Meeting and greeting

- The handshake is the most popular form of greeting.
- It is firm and quick, punctuated with a smile and the mention of your name.
- Shake hands with everyone individually, even children.

- Very close friends may greet each other with three air kisses near the cheeks, beginning with the left.
- Most Dutch people only use their first names around relatives and close friends.
- Do not use first names until you are invited to do so.

Gift-Giving Etiquette

- If invited to a Dutch house, bring a package of high-quality chocolates, a potted plant, a book, or flowers for the hostess.
- Flowers should be offered in odd numbers, not 13, as that is unlucky.
- Avoid presenting white flowers or chrysanthemums, which are linked with funerals.
- Gifts should be nicely wrapped.
- Wine is not a good gift when asked to dinner because the host may have already chosen the wines.
- Do not give pointy goods like knives or scissors because they are considered unlucky.
- When you receive a gift, you normally open it.

Dinner Etiquette

- The Netherlands has a somewhat formal dining culture.
- When dining, use the left hand for the fork and the right hand for the knife according to continental table etiquette.
- Remain standing until encouraged to sit. You may be shown to a certain seat. Men usually remain standing until all of the women have taken their seats.

- If you haven't finished your meal, cross your knife and fork in the center of the dish, with the fork over the knife.
- Don't start eating until the hostess does.
- Most meals, including sandwiches, are consumed with utensils.
- The host proposes the first toast. An honored visitor should repeat the toast later in the meal.
- Salad is not sliced; fold the lettuce with your fork.
- Always start with tiny portions so that you can accept second helpings.
- Finish everything on your platter. In the Netherlands, it is considered insulting to waste food.
- Lay your knife and fork parallel across the right side of your plate to indicate that you've finished eating.

Building Relationships and Communication

- Because of the country's long history of international trade, many Dutch are accustomed to doing business with foreigners.
- They will inquire about your academic credentials and the length of time your organization has been in existence.
- The corporate community is fairly close, and most senior executives know one another.
- Older, more bureaucratic companies may still judge you based on how you are introduced, therefore it is best to have a third-party introduction if feasible, though this is not required.
- The main thing is to illustrate how your partnership would benefit both parties.
- When it comes to business, the Dutch have a long-term perspective, so make sure your company's ambitions are clear.

- Because the Dutch cherish their time, do not expect them to work late or come in on weekends if you want to build a positive working relationship.
- The Dutch are hospitable, although this is usually saved for family and friends. In business, they are typically restrained and formal.
- They do not touch one another and like it when people they do business with keep the right distance, do not express emotion, or use dramatic hand movements.
- The Dutch are quite direct in their communication.
- They may sound brutal if you come from a culture where communication is more indirect and context-based.
- They do not employ hyperbole, and they expect to be told yes or no in simple language.
- In general, ideas will be addressed openly at meetings, with everyone allowed to voice their opinion.
- Information is shared throughout divisions, and business plans and goals are typically presented to all employees, particularly in more entrepreneurial companies.
- In these instances, decisions are frequently made based on consensus.
- Always appear modest and avoid making extravagant claims about what you or your firm can offer.
- Your word is your bond, and making claims that subsequently prove to be false will mark you as untrustworthy.

Explore AMSTERDAM | **169**

Outdoor Activities and Day Trips

Welcome to the green side of Amsterdam, where the cityscape transforms into a playground for natural wonders and outdoor activities. In this chapter, we invite you to swap hectic streets for peaceful parks, explore sparkling canals, and take day trips that offer a breath of fresh air. Whether you're a nature lover, a thrill-seeker, or simply looking to unwind beneath the stars, Amsterdam's outdoor attractions will captivate your senses and revitalize your spirit. Let's get outside and explore the lush landscapes, sparkling waters, and hidden gems in and around the wonderful city of Amsterdam.

Hand-Picked Cycling Routes

Why Rent a Bike?

The greatest way to get around in Amsterdam is undoubtedly by bicycle. There is a reason why there are two motorcycles for every inhabitant in the Netherlands! Every road in Amsterdam has a cycling path running beside it, and cyclists follow the same laws as vehicles. In addition, cycling from one side of Amsterdam to the other takes only 30 minutes, making it the shortest method to move about.

Cycle highways connect the entire Netherlands, making for an ideal cycling day excursion.

City Centre Route

This is an excellent cycle excursion if you don't want to drive far and want to visit some of the sights in Amsterdam's city center.

Distance - 29 kilometers

Time cycling - 2 hours

City Centre -> Cross the River IJ

Start at Discount Bike Rental and pedal north towards Centraal Station. The ferry terminals, located at the back of the station, allow passengers to board free passenger boats to the north of Amsterdam. Board the next ship sailing to Buiksloterweg.

- Once off the ferry, you have two options: visit the EYE Film Museum, which usually presents excellent exhibitions, or proceed directly to NDSM Wharf. NDSM, a former shipyard, is now a cultural hub for food, drink, events, art, and tourism on the banks of the River IJ. Park your bikes and explore.

NDSM-Wharf

Locate IJ-Hallen. Every three weeks, the largest flea market in Europe takes place on the NDSM pier, inside the enormous factory. It's ideal for anyone who appreciates finding bargains and visiting vintage markets. The entry fee is five euros.

Visit Pllek, a riverfront pub with a beach, outdoor beanbag lounging, beverages, and live music. The food is largely organic, made using fresh vegetables and local ingredients.

Or visit Noorderlicht next door, another riverbank tavern with outdoor seating, tasty food, and a relaxed/festival ambiance.

NDSM Wharf -> Vondelpark

Cycle to the nearest ferry station 'NDSM' and take the next ferry to Pontsteiger. From here, pedal south along Nassaukade for around 5 kilometers until you reach Vondelpark. This is a beautiful park to cycle through. Check out my post on Amsterdam Parks for some amazing drinking areas.

Vondelpark - Brouwerij 't IJ

Cycle from Vondelpark to Museumplein and via the Rijksmuseum to reach the historic Brouwerij 't IJ, which is only accessible to pedestrians and bikes. Then, turn right onto Stadhouderskade and ride along the canal rings, via the Heineken Experience and the Tropenmuseum (excellent attractions if you want to stop), and up to Brouwerij 't IJ.

Brouwerij 't IJ

Brouwerij 't IJ is a brewery located at Zeeburgerpad, tucked next to a huge windmill. The structure was once a bathhouse, as evidenced by the original tiles and soap holders beneath one of the fermentation tanks, as well as the male and female change signs over the tasting room entrance. The beers are excellent; I recommend a flight of beers with some borrelhapjes ("drink snacks"). Furthermore, if you plan it correctly, they provide 20-minute guided tours in English at 3:30 pm on Friday, Saturday, and Sunday for 6.50 euros.

From here, I'd cycle back to Amsterdam's center, passing Centraal Station before turning left back into the city center. This ride covers approximately 30 kilometers and takes about 2 hours to complete.

Amsterdam Woodland Route

This cycle route runs through the city center and south to Amsterdamse Bos ('Amsterdam Woods'). It is a nice in-between route because it contains landmarks in the city center as well as parks and green space. If the weather is nice, you can go swimming and sunbathing!

Distance - 29 kilometers

Time spent cycling: approximately 2 hours.

Amsterdam Canals -> Woodland

Starting in the center (I'm using Discount Bike Rental as a starting point), pedal towards the 9 Straatjes, the lovely streets nestled among a network of canals. You'll pass Pluk (a trendy cafe with cakes, yogurt bowls, and healthy food) and The Houseboat Museum (visit a traditional Dutch houseboat for 4.50 euros) if you want to stop.

- Continue cycling south, towards Amsterdamse Bos. You'll cross Vondelpark, then pass Museumplein on your left, where you can see the Stedelijk Museum and the Rijksmuseum, before passing through the upscale neighborhood of South Amsterdam. Just before reaching Amterdamse Bos, you'll have the opportunity to stop by the XL Albert Heijn store to pick up food and drinks for a picnic.

Amsterdamse Bos

You can enter Amsterdamse Bos through the entry near de Boswinkle. Once in the park area, there are numerous cycle lanes to explore and activities to enjoy. Cycle through vast woodlands, past blossoming trees, and lakes. If you want to swim, there are two open-air pools plus a few cafes and restaurants.

Back to the Centre

After exploring Amsterdamse Bos, you can cycle back to the center of Amsterdam. Taking a different route back will take you past the Olympic Stadium and via Vondelpark.

The cycle route concludes with a 10-minute return to the city center via Food Hallen. If you're hungry, go to Food Hallen, an enormous indoor food hall with hundreds of street food options, a gin and tonic bar, and live DJs on the nights (I highly recommend the Vietnamese banh-mi sandwich and the prawn tempura bun!).

Water Activities

Amsterdam is a city of water, so there are numerous ways to make the most of living near canals, rivers, and lakes. The water in Amsterdam is rather clean, and the authorities inspect the condition of the water in recreational lakes every two weeks.

Hire a Boat

Hiring your boat and taking a tour of the canals is something I highly recommend doing when in Amsterdam. Renting a boat for 2-3 hours costs roughly €100 and can often accommodate up to 8 persons. In the past, I used Mokumboot; they have cheap costs and all of their boats are electric, which is better for the environment. You do not need a license to captain one of these boats, and they are incredibly easy to maneuver!

We would normally go to the grocery and grab some crates of beer and picnic food before getting on the boat. There are a few rules for boats on the canals, such as staying to the right and not playing loud music.

Amsterdam offers numerous boat-accessible bars and pubs, ideal for purchasing additional beverages or using the restroom.

- Hannekes Boom
- Waterkant
- Edel
- Zouthaven
- Loetje aan 't IJ

Stand-Up Paddleboarding (SUP)

Sloterplas is an excellent site to go stand-up paddle boarding in Amsterdam. This lake, located in Sloterpark, has a water facility perched on the edge where you may rent water sports equipment. If you rent paddle boards for more than two hours, you may paddle from the watersports facility to Sloterplas Beach, a sandy urban beach with eateries and a volleyball net.

Watersport Centrum Sloterplas rents SUP boards for €15 per hour and kayaks for €7.50 per hour.

Visit the Beach

If you want to go surfing, you'll need to travel further away to the nearest beach, Zandvoort. This vast sandy beach is 34 minutes by train from Amsterdam, so plan on spending the majority of your day there. But once you're there, there's much to do, including:

- Surfing, stand-up paddleboarding, and kitesurfing.
- Swim in the sea.
- Visit one of its 30 beach clubs.

First Wave Surf School offers surfboard and wetsuit rentals for €12.50 per hour.

Open Water Swimming

There are some wonderful open-water swimming sites in and around Amsterdam. Check out the following.

Sloterplas is one of the best places to swim, with an urban sandy beach on the edge of a lake that is ideal for swimming, picnics, and volleyball.

Amsterdamse Bos - In Amsterdam's largest landscape park, there are various areas to swim, notably Grote Vijver (Big Pond).

IJBurg is an eastern Amsterdam suburb featuring a sandy man-made beach ideal for picnics and swimming.

Canal Kayak or SUP Tours

See Amsterdam from the canals on your kayak or paddleboard, an enjoyable pastime for a bright summer day! Rent stand-up paddleboards, kayaks, canoes, and wetsuits from https://kanoensupamsterdam.nl/

You can either rent the equipment on an hourly basis and go out on your own, or you can join one of their group excursions.

Explore AMSTERDAM | 179

Windmills and Tulip Fields

Amsterdam's downtown was once clogged with windmills serving a variety of functions, from avoiding flooding to grinding the seeds for the Dutch favorite condiment, mustard. The majority of the capital's windmills have since been removed, but eight remain. As it turns out, windmills have been on the move, and many of Amsterdam's mills have been relocated to the outskirts, where wind conditions are more favorable than in the densely populated center city. While only the Molen van Sloten is open to the public, many mills participate in National Windmill Day, which takes place on the second Saturday in May and turns these old structures into bustling hives of activity once more.

The outdoor museum Zaanse Schans, located just outside of Amsterdam, has many windmills to admire. It honors the Dutch tradition, which was once peppered with 10,000 windmills.

Windmills in Amsterdam

Molen van Sloten

The Sloten Windmill is the only one of Amsterdam's eight windmills exposed to the public. It is still operational, and as a draining mill or tjasker, it is used to pump surplus water from the surrounding area, which was originally known as Haarlemmer Lake.

Akersluis 10

020 669 0412

molenvansloten.nl

Open every day from 10 a.m. to 4.30 p.m. (closed on January 1, April 27, and December 25 and 26)

De Gooyer

Visit de Gooyer mill to accomplish two goals at once. If you do, you will not only visit Amsterdam's most iconic mill, but you will also be able to enjoy one of the city's best beers, brewed next door at the 't IJ brewery. The mill, erected in 1725, is the highest wooden mill in the Netherlands. It was utilized as a corn mill during its working life, but it has not been operational since 1972 when it was damaged by a storm.

Funenkade 5

De Otter

De Otter, a small paltrok mill, is not far from De Bloem. Built in 1631 as one of many sawmills in the area, it operated until the early 1900s. Due to Amsterdam's expanding population and industrialization, all save the Otter sawmill were demolished. The mill was restored to full working order in the 1990s; however, the numerous structures that have sprung up in the region mean that wind conditions are no longer adequate for operating the mill. As a result, the owners proposed relocating the mill, but because it is a national monument, they needed to obtain approval from the municipal council. Several court cases later, the Otter remains in its current site.

Gillis Van Ledenberchstraat 78

Riekermolen

No mill in Amsterdam appears to be permanently rooted in place, and the Riekermolen is no exception. Built-in 1636 in the village of Sloten, just outside Amsterdam, the Riekermill was relocated to its current location next to the Amstel River in 1961. It is a drainage mill, similar to the Molen van Sloten, but unlike its operational counterpart, it has been retired. Nonetheless, when the wind is perfect, the Riekermolen continues to spin on weekends in the afternoon. Next to it, there is a statue of Rembrandt, who loved this location and immortalized it in many of his sketches.

De Borcht 10 is open on various weekends from 12 noon until 5 pm.

D'Admiraal

Take the ferry to Amsterdam Noord to see the last chalk and trass mill in the Netherlands. Built-in 1792 to grind a volcanic stone from the German Eifel region for mortar production, it was later used to crush chalk for putty. It was built (and remains) in the scenic Buiksloot, a former village that is now part of Amsterdam.

Noordhollandskanaaldijk 21

De Bloem

Flour mill de Bloem, built in 1768, began operations on the Bloemgracht in the Jordaan. Much like the de Gooyer windmill, it was eventually moved to a more windy place on the outskirts of town. Today it serves as an office and can only be visited on National Windmill Day.

Haarlemmerweg 465

Windmills on Just Outside of Amsterdam

De Zaanse Schans

Can't get enough of windmills or Dutch history? Then Zaanse Schans is the right spot for you. Zaanse Schans, an outdoor museum, is located just a short train ride from Amsterdam. Since 1961, old mills, buildings, and barns from the 18th and 19th centuries have been transferred to this area outside Zaandam, resulting in a lively village and a living monument.

The Zaanse Schans is home to eight windmills with fantastic names like The Cat (de-cat), The Spotted Hen (de bonte hen), and The Cloverleaf (het klaverblad). The mills served a variety of functions, including sawmills, oil mills, and mustard mills. With so many other attractions at the Zaanse Schans (including a bakery museum and a museum of Dutch clocks), you could easily spend the entire day exploring the region.

Schansend 7, Zaandam - dezaanseschans.nl.

Open: Monday through Sunday, 10 a.m. to 5 p.m.

The Netherlands is well-known around the world as one of the best sites to see and enjoy tulips. Its sprawling tulip fields, lined with rows of brightly colored flowers, are one of the country's biggest attractions, drawing millions of visitors throughout their peak season.

Find a detailed guide to all of the top Netherlands tulip fields, including when to visit and other suggestions!

Best Tulip Fields in the Netherlands

Noordoostpolder

Noordoostpolder is one of the best spots in the Netherlands to see stunning rows of tulips. It is located in the Flevoland area of the Netherlands, which is home to some of the country's best and most stunning tulip fields. The best site in this province to see the magnificent fields of tulips is Noordoostpolder.

Noordoostpolder is located further away from the more prominent cities in the Netherlands, thus they are less touristy and more pleasurable as a result. With almost 5,000 acres of rainbow-colored fields, it is Holland's largest flower-growing region and a must-see destination. In addition, a specific Tulip Route is mapped for visitors each year!

Pros

– Largest tulip-growing region in Holland

– Can explore by car or bike

– Less touristy

Cons

– Far from many big cities in Holland

Schagen

Schagen is a little village in North Holland with rows of beautiful tulip fields. The famous Dutch windmills in the background are what make these tulip fields so appealing. This simply adds to the attractiveness of the tulip fields, making it feel like the quintessential Dutch experience.

These fields are slightly more remote than others, requiring a car or public transportation to get there. To get to these fields from Amsterdam, plan on driving for an hour and taking public transportation for more than an hour. After that, you'll have to cycle to get there and explore. You can either bring your bike on the train or hire one in town.

Cycle from Schagen to Moerbeek for a complete tour of the tulips. Because they are considered more remote, you will have the opportunity to appreciate these fields alone!

Pros

Beautiful fields

Traditional Dutch windmills in the background

Less busy

Cons

Far from Amsterdam

Requires a bike

The Bollenstreek: Lisse/Hillegom/Noorwijkerhout

The Bollenstreek is a region in Western Holland famed for its picturesque flower meadows. It is undoubtedly one of the most popular and touristy Dutch tulip fields, but it is also one of the best. Due to its popularity, it is preferable to visit early in the morning or during the week to avoid crowds.

The popularity of these tulip fields can be attributed in part to their location. It is a convenient field for everyone because it is centrally placed in the Netherlands and is easily accessible from all major cities. If you want to catch a train with your bike already on board or easily locate a variety of bike rental firms, here is the field for you!

Pros

– *Conveniently located in the middle of The Netherlands*

– *Easy to reach*

– *Can explore by bike or car*

Cons

– *One of the Netherlands' most popular tourist destinations*

– *Very busy on weekends*

Goeree-Overflakkee

Goeree-Overflakkee is a hidden gem in the Netherlands, ideal for anyone wishing to explore some gorgeous Dutch tulip fields with no one else around. Goeree-Overflakkee's tulip fields are just as magnificent and vivid as those elsewhere in the country, but they are more undisturbed.

The best way to reach here is by automobile, where you may see and photograph the fields along the road. Tulip fields are most abundant in the areas surrounding Middelharnis and Dirksland.

Pros

– *Off the beaten path*

– *Few other people*

Cons

– *Must reach these fields by car*

Keukenhof

Keukenhof is regarded as the world's most beautiful flower garden. Every year, millions of tourists visit these gardens, eager to view the amazing flower arrangements and gardens. Although there are no tulip fields here, it is an excellent spot to visit if you want to see a variety of flowers and art installations.

Make sure to get your tickets in advance and try to visit during the week, as weekends are extremely packed.

How to Get to Tulip Fields

The best way to get to all of the Netherlands' tulip fields is by vehicle. Renting a car allows you to quickly get to all of the fields (which are not in town) and travel between them.

Another option is to take public transportation. This alternative may be challenging for some fields that demand frequent train changes and other enterprises.

You will need a bicycle to navigate around the fields! Rent a bike or bring one with you; this is the best way to enjoy the whole experience.

Dutch Tulip Fields Season

The tulip season in the Netherlands runs from **late March to early May.** This is the only time of year to visit the Netherlands and view all of the beautiful and iconic tulip fields in full bloom.

The window of opportunity to appreciate the fields is rather narrow, but with appropriate planning, you should have no problems.

Please keep in mind that blooming times may vary based on the time of year and conditions. For example, it could be a cold spring that results in a late bloom season, with tulips blooming brilliantly in April.

On the other hand, it could be a scorching spring, with tulip fields plowed and beginning to wilt in early May.

As a result, mid-April is the finest time to visit the Netherlands' tulip fields.

Tulip Field Tips

- Bring or rent a bicycle.
- Pack food and beverages.
- Make sure your camera and phone are updated.
- Plan your route.
- Understand that the field sites change each year! Farmers cannot plant in the same spot year after year since it is bad for the flowers, which will change.

Explore AMSTERDAM | **191**

Ice Skating

If you visit Amsterdam in the winter, you'll probably discover that the Dutch enjoy ice skating. When the temperatures dip low enough, the canals freeze over, and many Dutch residents will go to the ice with their skates to zoom up and down the canals.

If you don't want to take a chance on the canals, you may rent skates and swoop around the ice at one of the other gorgeous locations.

Rijksmuseum

Perhaps one of the most popular venues to rent skates is the Rijksmuseum. This temporary rink is set up at Museumplein from November to early February each year, with the museum serving as a beautiful backdrop.

Brasserie Winters, a wooden chalet near the rink, serves a variety of Dutch and international dishes. You may buy glouwijn (mulled wine) or beer and watch the skaters from the bridge, which is my favorite way to enjoy ice skating.

Ice Rink Rembrandtplein

This temporary ice rink is located on Rembrandtplein, a bustling drinking area, and is flanked by wooden kiosks selling food, beverages, and Christmas-themed items.

Canals

During colder winters Amsterdam's famed canals will periodically freeze over producing a really lovely scenery and an area suited for ice skating. The temperature must remain below -4 degrees Celsius for four nights in a row, after which the council closes off particular canals and allows them to freeze for ice skating!

Many Amsterdam residents own their ice skates. If you can find some, perhaps from one of the daily markets or Dutch sports shops, you'll have a one-of-a-kind opportunity to skate down the canals.

Sporting Events and Venues

Every year, Amsterdam hosts some of the world's most prestigious sporting events, including darts and tennis, marathons, and football. If you want to combine your trip to Amsterdam with a sporting event, take a look at the events listed below.

Ajax

Ajax Amsterdam Football Club (AFC) Ajax was formed in March 1900 and is historically one of the world's most successful clubs, one of just five to have earned the privilege of retaining the European Cup.

The stadium is located 15 minutes via metro from Amsterdam Centraal. You may take the World of Ajax tour and visit the Ajax Museum at the stadium, or if you're in Amsterdam on a match day, go and watch. The Johan Cruijff ArenA seats 55,000 people, and the Dutch create a pleasant atmosphere.

Amsterdam City Swim

The City Swim is an annual event held in September to raise funds for motor neuron disease (ALS in the Netherlands).

Swimmers generally start at the Marine Etablissement Amsterdam and swim the 2,000-meter route, which ends on the Keizersgracht.

You can give, swim, or simply watch, with entertainment usually provided around the start and finish lines.

TCS Amsterdam Marathon

The Amsterdam Marathon, which begins and ends at the Olympic Stadium, takes place every October. The path includes various landmarks along the way, including the Rijksmuseum, the Zuidas, the river Amstel, and a trip through Vondelpark.

If you want to go and watch, the atmosphere is fantastic, and if you're a runner, you can compete in the marathon, half marathon, or 8km.

Practical Tips and Resources

As you begin your Amsterdam adventure, it's time to empower yourself with the insider knowledge that elevates a good vacation to an extraordinary one. In this section, we'll get into the practical details, ensuring that your experience is smooth, entertaining, and full of insider information. From safety tips to cultural etiquette, and language tidbits to must-have apps, consider this your backstage pass to mastering the art of exploring Amsterdam like a seasoned explorer. So, fasten your seatbelts, because the practical adventure begins!

Safety and Health Information

Amsterdam is a safe destination to visit. Pick-pocketing will be your main concern, and it commonly occurs on crowded public transportation. Keep your belongings secure at all times, and keep valuables tucked away for safety. Don't flaunt your valuables, either.

As a notorious party city, robbers can easily take advantage of drunk travelers at night. Keep your stuff nearby and keep an eye on your drink. To stay safe, do not accept alcohol from strangers, and avoid being very inebriated.

The Red Light District has gotten more dangerous in recent years, as illegal substances and violent crime have increased. Keep an eye out while you're there.

There are a few frequent scams in Amsterdam, such as persons offering to sell you used public transit tickets. Be wary of buying a particularly cheap bike from someone on the street, as it is likely to be stolen.

Solo female travelers should feel comfortable here. However, typical precautions apply (never leave your drink unattended at the bar, never go home intoxicated alone at night, etc.), especially since this is a party city. Keep an eye on your drinks. There are other single-female blogs out there that can offer more specific advice based on their experience.

If you have an emergency, call 112 for help.

Always follow your gut inclination. Make copies of your documents, such as your passport and ID. Give loved ones a copy of your itinerary so they can follow your whereabouts.

The most crucial advice I can give is to have good travel insurance. Travel insurance protects you from illness, injury, theft, and cancellation. It provides comprehensive protection if something goes wrong. I never go without it because I've had to use it several times in the past.

Essential Dutch Phrases

As a general rule, I generally recommend that travelers learn some basic local terminology. First, not everyone understands English or your original language. Second, people enjoy it when visitors make an effort to speak their language. It's a great approach to begin a pleasant interaction!

Here are some crucial Dutch words and phrases to master before your trip to Amsterdam:

Basic Greetings:

1. Hello - Hallo
2. Goodbye - Tot ziens
3. Please - Alsjeblieft (informal) / Alsjeblieft (formal)
4. Thank you - Dank je (informal) / Dank u (formal)
5. Excuse me - Pardon

Common Phrases: 6. Yes - Ja

7. No - Nee
8. I don't understand - Ik begrijp het niet
9. Can you help me? - Kun je me helpen?
10. I'm lost - Ik ben verdwaald
11. Where is...? - Waar is...?
12. How much does this cost? - Hoeveel kost dit?
13. What time is it? - Hoe laat is het?
14. Do you speak English? - Spreek je Engels?

Directions: 15. Left - Links

16. Right - Rechts

17. Straight ahead - Rechtdoor

18. Map - Kaart

Transportation: 19. Train station - Treinstation

20. Bus station - Busstation

21. Tram - Tram

22. Metro - Metro

23. Taxi - Taxi

Food and Drinks: 24. Restaurant - Restaurant

25. Cafe - Café

26. Menu - Menu

27. Water - Water

28. Beer - Bier

29. Coffee - Koffie

30. Tea - Thee

Numbers: 31. One - Een

32. Two - Twee

33. Three - Drie

34. Four - Vier

35. Five - Vijf

Emergency Phrases: 36. Help! - Hulp!

37. Police - Politie

38. Doctor - Dokter

39. I need assistance - Ik heb hulp nodig

These phrases should help you handle basic exchanges and get around Amsterdam more easily. Remember, while many Dutch people speak English fluently, making an effort to speak Dutch is always appreciated!

Photography Tips

Amsterdam is a stunning and scenic city that provides numerous opportunities for excellent photography. Here are some crucial photographic recommendations for tourists visiting Amsterdam:

Golden Hour Magic: Capture the city during the golden hour, which occurs after sunrise and before sunset. The soft, warm light at these times might improve your images and create a magical mood.

Canal Reflections: Make use of the renowned waterways. Capture the reflections of houses, boats, and bridges on the lake to create magnificent scenes.

Bicycles Everywhere: Amsterdam is referred to be the "City of Bikes." Include bicycles in your photographs to convey a sense of local life and culture. Look for streets and bridges that are lined with bicycles.

Classic Amsterdam houses: Take photos of the unusual and narrow canal houses. Experiment with various angles and viewpoints to highlight their architecture. The Jordaan and Grachtengordel neighborhoods are very attractive.

Famous landmarks: Don't miss out on capturing prominent locations like the Anne Frank House, Rijksmuseum, Van Gogh Museum, and Amsterdam Sign. Experiment with various perspectives and compositions.

Street Photography: Explore the lovely streets and alleyways. Candid photos of inhabitants, street performers, and everyday life can convey a true sense of the city.

Tulip and Flower Markets: If you go in the spring, don't miss the spectacular tulip displays in parks like Keukenhof and the floating flower market. The colors create very beautiful photos.

Amsterdam At Night: Capture the city's nightlife, particularly in the Red Light district. The brightly lit canals and bridges provide a distinct perspective after dark.

Museums and galleries: Many museums and galleries in Amsterdam include remarkable architecture. Photograph the exteriors and interiors of these cultural sites.

Boat tours: Take a canal boat excursion to get a unique perspective on the city. Photograph the metropolis from the sea, including both iconic and hidden jewels.

People and Local Cultures: Engage with the people and capture moments that highlight Amsterdam's culture and variety. When photographing close-up photographs, always respect people's privacy and ask permission beforehand.

Weather Preparedness: Be prepared for different weather situations. Amsterdam can be rainy, so bring rain gear for your photography. Additionally, gloomy skies can add drama to your photographs.

Explore the Neighborhoods: Go beyond the city core. Each district in Amsterdam has its distinct charm and character, providing several photo opportunities.

When photographing people, remember to respect their privacy and the local customs. These suggestions should help you capture the beauty and essence of Amsterdam during your visit.

Useful Apps and Websites

When traveling, safety is a primary consideration, and there are various handy applications and websites to assist tourists stay safe in Amsterdam. Here are some crucial safety applications and websites for people visiting Amsterdam:

1. **Google Maps:**

    - **Website:** https://maps.google.com

    - **App:** Google Maps (iOS, Android)

    - Google Maps is essential for navigation, helping you find your way around the city, locate landmarks, and plan routes while it also provides real-time traffic updates and public transportation information.

2. **Amsterdam & Region Travel Ticket App:**

    - **Website:** www.gvb.nl/en/

    - **App:** GVB Tickets (iOS, Android)

    - This app allows you to purchase and store public transportation tickets for trams, buses, and metro in Amsterdam because it's convenient for getting around the city.

3. **112 Netherlands:**

    - **Website:** Emergency Number 112

- **App:** Emergency Number 112 (iOS, Android)
- In case of emergencies, the 112 app provides quick access to emergency services because it's the universal emergency number in the Netherlands.

4. **Amsterdam Police:**
   - **Website:** www.politie.nl/en
   - The official website of the Dutch police provides information on safety, reporting crimes, and contacting the police if needed.

5. **Smart Traveler:**
   - **Website:** https://step.state.gov/
   - If you're a U.S. citizen, consider enrolling in the Smart Traveler program. In the event of an emergency, it enables communication between you and the U.S. Embassy and offers safety updates.

6. **Travel Insurance Provider App:**
   - If you have travel insurance, make sure to download the app provided by your insurance company. It can be useful for accessing emergency contacts, policy information, and filing claims.

7. **Weather Apps:**
   - Stay informed about the weather conditions in Amsterdam. Apps like AccuWeather, The Weather Channel, or your preferred weather app can help you plan your activities accordingly.

8. **Travel Safe Abroad:**

    - **Website:** www.travelsafe-abroad.com

    - For U.S. citizens, the U.S. Department of State provides country-specific travel information, including safety and security details for the Netherlands.

Please keep in mind that app availability may differ depending on your device's app store, therefore you can search for the apps directly in the iOS App Store or Google Play Store using the app names provided.

To guarantee a safe and pleasurable journey, always remain cautious, aware of your surroundings, and adhere to local guidelines. Check for updates or new safety apps closer to your travel date, as technology and advice may change.

Explore AMSTERDAM | **205**

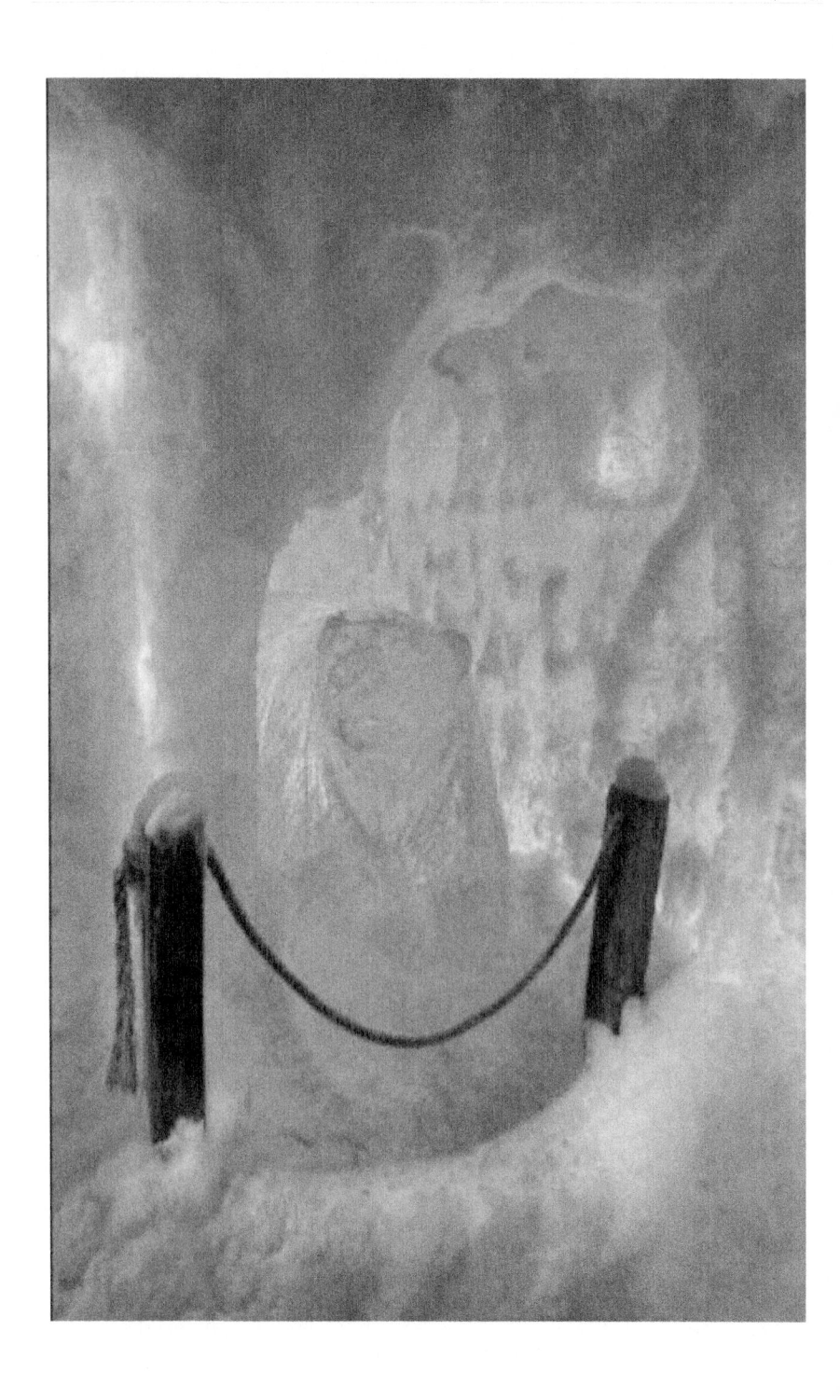

The Best Booking Resources

These are my favorite brands to utilize while traveling. They continuously deliver the best prices, world-class customer service, and outstanding value, and outperform their competitors. They are the firms I use the most and always start with when looking for vacation offers.

Skyscanner - This is my favorite flight search engine. They look for smaller websites and low-cost airlines that major search engines sometimes overlook because they are unquestionably the best place to start.

(http://tinyurl.com/ytw4ut9k)

Hostelworld - This is the best hostel lodging website out there, with the largest inventory, the best search interface, and the most availability.

(http://tinyurl.com/5a27cs6t)

Booking.com - is the greatest all-around booking service, consistently offering the cheapest and lowest rates. They have the most affordable accommodation options. In all of my tests, they consistently offered the lowest rates of any booking website.

(www.booking.com)

Get Your Guide - is a large online marketplace for tours and excursions. They provide a wide range of tour alternatives in cities across the world, including cooking classes, walking tours, street art lessons, and more!

(www.getyourguide.com)

SafetyWing - Safety Wing provides convenient and inexpensive plans designed for digital nomads and long-term travelers. They provide low-cost monthly plans, excellent customer service, and an easy-to-use claims process, making it ideal for individuals on the go.

(www.safetywing.com)

LifeStraw - is my go-to company for reusable water bottles with built-in filters, ensuring your drinking water is always pure and safe.

(http://tinyurl.com/25wzfs2m)

Unbound Merino - manufactures lightweight, durable, and easy-to-clean travel clothes.

(www.unboundmerino.com)

Top Travel Credit Cards - Points are the most effective strategy to reduce travel expenses. Here are my best credit cards for accumulating points and getting free trips!

(www.nomadicmatt.com)

BlaBlaCar - BlaBlaCar is a ridesharing website that allows you to share rides with vetted local drivers in exchange for gas. You simply request a seat, they approve, and you're off! It's a more affordable and entertaining way to travel than taking the bus or the train!

(www.blablacar.com)

Conclusion

As we say goodbye to the colorful city of Amsterdam, we hope this book has been a reliable companion in discovering the mysteries of this amazing place. From iconic canals to hidden treasures, and cultural indulgences to outdoor adventures, your tour has been a tapestry of wonderful experiences.

We hope Amsterdam's charm has left an everlasting stamp on your heart, and that the experiences curated within these pages have given a distinct hue to your travel palette. As you keep these memories with you, may they serve as a reminder of the beauty that exists in every corner of the earth.

Remember that Amsterdam is more than just a city; it is a vibe, an environment, and a collection of stories ready to be told. Whether you return to its cobbled streets or go off on a new adventure, may your journey be filled with joy, curiosity, and amazement.

Farewell, lovely traveler. Until the next voyage, wherever it leads, may it be as magical as your time in Amsterdam. Safe travels!

Itinerary

3day Itinerary

Day 1: Historic Charm and Canal Strolls

Morning

- **9:00 AM - 10:30 AM:** Begin your day at Dam Square, the heart of Amsterdam. Explore the Royal Palace and the National Monument. Enjoy a leisurely breakfast at a nearby café.

Late Morning

- **11:00 AM - 1:00 PM:** Head to the Anne Frank House. Book tickets in advance to avoid queues. Immerse yourself in the poignant history of Anne Frank and World War II.

Afternoon

- **1:30 PM - 3:00 PM:** Grab lunch in the Jordaan district, known for its charming streets and unique boutiques. Afterward, take a relaxing canal cruise to see the city from a different perspective.

Late Afternoon

- **3:30 PM - 5:00 PM:** Explore the Rijksmuseum, home to a vast collection of Dutch art and history. Don't miss the famous "Night Watch."

Evening

- **6:30 PM onwards:** Enjoy dinner at a traditional Dutch restaurant in De Pijp. Take a stroll through the neighborhood's vibrant streets.

Day 2: Cultural Delights and Hidden Gems

Morning

- **9:30 AM - 11:00 AM:** Begin your day at the Van Gogh Museum. Marvel at the masterpieces of this iconic artist.

Late Morning

- **11:30 AM - 1:00 PM:** Explore the Albert Cuyp Market in De Pijp. Indulge in regional cuisine and souvenir shopping.

Afternoon

- **1:30 PM - 3:00 PM:** Visit the Vondelpark for a family picnic. Rent bikes for a scenic ride through the park.

Late Afternoon

- **3:30 PM - 5:00 PM:** Head to the NEMO Science Museum for interactive exhibits suitable for all ages.

Evening

- **6:30 PM onwards:** Dine at a waterside restaurant in the Red Light District. Take an evening stroll through this historic area.

Day 3: Nature Retreat and Authentic Dutch Experience

Morning

- **10:00 AM - 11:30 AM:** Take a day trip to Keukenhof Gardens to immerse yourself in vibrant tulip fields (seasonal).

Late Morning

- **12:00 PM - 1:30 PM:** Enjoy lunch in the nearby town of Haarlem. Explore its historic streets and landmarks.

Afternoon

- **2:00 PM - 4:00 PM:** Return to Amsterdam and visit the Rembrandt House Museum to discover the life and art of the renowned painter.

Late Afternoon

- **4:30 PM - 6:00 PM:** Wrap up your trip at the Zaanse Schans for a taste of Dutch windmills and traditional crafts.

Evening

- **7:00 PM onwards:** Conclude your Amsterdam adventure with a farewell dinner at a canal-side restaurant, reminiscing about the wonderful memories created during your family getaway.

7 day Itinerary

Here's a full 7-day schedule for a family-friendly visit to Amsterdam, with suggested activities, sites, and approximate periods for each day:

Day 1: Getting Acquainted with Amsterdam

- Morning (9:00 AM - 12:00 PM): Arrive and settle into your accommodation.

- Afternoon (1:00 PM - 4:00 PM): Explore Dam Square and visit the Royal Palace.

- Evening (6:00 PM - 8:00 PM): Dinner in the Jordaan district, known for its charming streets and local eateries.

Day 2: Cultural Immersion

- Morning (9:00 AM - 12:00 PM): Rijksmuseum visit – delve into Dutch art and history.

- Afternoon (1:00 PM - 4:00 PM): Stroll through the nearby Vondelpark, a perfect spot for a family picnic.

- Evening (6:00 PM - 8:00 PM): Enjoy a canal cruise to witness the city from a different perspective.

Day 3: Family Fun in Amsterdam

- Morning (9:00 AM - 12:00 PM): Visit the interactive NEMO Science Museum, perfect for kids.

- Afternoon (1:00 PM - 4:00 PM): Head to Artis Royal Zoo for a family-friendly animal encounter.

- Evening (6:00 PM - 8:00 PM): Relax at a family-friendly restaurant in the Plantage district.

Day 4: Exploring Quirky Amsterdam

- Morning (9:00 AM - 12:00 PM): Discover Anne Frank House (book tickets in advance).

- Afternoon (1:00 PM - 4:00 PM): Meander through the De Pijp neighborhood, known for its eclectic atmosphere.

- Evening (6:00 PM - 8:00 PM): Enjoy dinner at a cozy café on Utrechtsestraat.

Day 5: Outdoor Adventure

- Morning (9:00 AM - 12:00 PM): Rent bikes and explore Amsterdam's bike-friendly paths.

- Afternoon (1:00 PM - 4:00 PM): Visit Keukenhof Gardens (seasonal), known for its breathtaking tulip displays.

- Evening (6:00 PM - 8:00 PM): Return to the city and dine in a canal-side restaurant.

Day 6: Day Trip to Zaanse Schans

- Full Day Excursion (9:00 AM - 6:00 PM): Take a day trip to Zaanse Schans, a charming village with traditional windmills, crafts, and Dutch heritage. Return in the evening for dinner in Amsterdam.

Day 7: Relax and Explore

- Morning (9:00 AM - 12:00 PM): Enjoy a leisurely morning in Vondelpark or visit the Van Gogh Museum.

- Afternoon (1:00 PM - 4:00 PM): Explore the shopping district around Kalverstraat.

- Evening (6:00 PM - 8:00 PM): Conclude your trip with a farewell dinner in the atmospheric Jordaan district.

Feel free to change the itinerary according to your family's tastes and the time of year. It is recommended that you get tickets in advance for popular attractions to ensure a seamless and enjoyable trip.

14day Itinerary

Day 1-2: Arrival and Canal Cruise

- **Day 1:**

    - Morning: Arrive in Amsterdam, and check into accommodation.

    - Afternoon: Explore Dam Square and the Royal Palace.

    - Evening: Stroll along the iconic canals, and have dinner at a canal-side restaurant.

- **Day 2:**

    - Morning: Visit Anne Frank House (book tickets in advance).

    - Afternoon: Take a relaxing canal cruise to get acquainted with the city.

    - Evening: Explore the Jordaan district, known for its trendy shops and cafes.

Day 3-4: Cultural Immersion

- **Day 3:**

    - Morning: Visit the Rijksmuseum (book tickets in advance).

    - Afternoon: Explore the Van Gogh Museum.

    - Evening: Enjoy a leisurely dinner in Leidseplein.

- **Day 4:**

- Morning: Discover the historic Begijnhof.
- Afternoon: Visit the Rembrandt House Museum.
- Evening: Attend a live performance at the Concertgebouw.

Day 5-7: Family Fun

- Day 5:
    - Morning: Explore NEMO Science Museum.
    - Afternoon: Visit ARTIS Amsterdam Royal Zoo.
    - Evening: Relax in Vondelpark.
- Day 6:
    - Day Trip: Keukenhof Gardens and Tulip Fields (seasonal).
    - Evening: Return to Amsterdam for a family dinner.
- Day 7:
    - Morning: Enjoy a family bike ride through Amsterdam.
    - Afternoon: Visit the Amsterdam Museum.
    - Evening: Try a Dutch pancake dinner in De Pijp.

Day 8-10: Outdoor Adventures

- Day 8:
    - Morning: Day trip to Zaanse Schans for windmills and Dutch crafts.

- Afternoon: Explore the nearby town of Haarlem.
- Evening: Return to Amsterdam for dinner.

- **Day 9:**
  - Morning: Rent a boat for a family canal adventure.
  - Afternoon: Visit the Hortus Botanicus Amsterdam.
  - Evening: Relax in a canal-side cafe.

- **Day 10:**
  - Morning: Discover the A'DAM Lookout and Over the Edge Swing.
  - Afternoon: Take a ferry to NDSM Wharf for street art.
  - Evening: Savor a meal at a restaurant beside the water.

Day 11-14: Leisure and Shopping

- **Day 11:**
  - Morning: Leisurely breakfast and visit Bloemenmarkt (Flower Market).
  - Afternoon: Shopping in Nine Streets (De Negen Straatjes).
  - Evening: Canal-side dinner in the Red Light District.

- **Day 12:**
  - Morning: Visit the Heineken Experience.
  - Afternoon: Free time for leisure or optional activities.

- Evening: Attend a family-friendly show at Boom Chicago.

- **Day 13:**

  - Morning: Explore the Amsterdam Dungeon for a unique experience.

  - Afternoon: Shopping in Kalverstraat.

  - Evening: Farewell dinner in a local favorite restaurant.

- **Day 14: Departure**

  - Morning: Last-minute souvenir shopping.

  - Afternoon: Check out and leave for the airport.

This schedule combines cultural research, family-friendly events, outdoor experiences, and relaxation time to provide a well-rounded experience for families visiting Amsterdam. Remember to check the opening hours and availability of attractions ahead of time, and feel free to modify the itinerary based on your family's tastes and the season of your visit.

Frequently Asked Questions

How Many Days in Amsterdam Is Sufficient?

As usual, visitors to Amsterdam spend two to four days visiting the city's major sights, sampling Dutch cuisine, and enjoying the city. If you intend to take day trips, make sure to remain longer.

How much should I budget for Amsterdam?

A three-day vacation to Amsterdam will cost $220 if you're traveling alone, $2070 if you're traveling with a partner, and $2680 if you're traveling with a family of four. Hotel costs in the city center range from $370 to $950 (the average is $475 per night). It is recommended that you set about $135 per day per person for eating out and transportation.

Finally, keep in mind that your expenses will vary based on the type of accommodation you choose, the length of your visit, and how you spend your money once there. The budget calculations listed above are based on prior guests' experiences and are just intended to provide you with an overall sense of your likely spending.

Do People Tip in Amsterdam?

While there is no official regulation requiring you to tip, it is advised that you give a small tip (5-10% of the total price) if you are satisfied with the service. If the service was average, feel free to round up the bill.

Can You Make a Day Journey from Amsterdam to Paris?

Yes, you can take a day's journey from Amsterdam to Paris. It takes roughly three hours by train. However, while it is technically possible to visit Paris, you will not be able to see everything in one day. Paris is such a large city that visitors can easily stay for a week and have something different to do every day.

When is the ideal time to visit Amsterdam?

The best time to visit Amsterdam is in the spring (April to May) when the tulips are in bloom, or in the late summer (September) when the weather is good and there are fewer tourists.

Is it required to buy an Amsterdam card?

The I Amsterdam Card can be used for free public transportation, museum admission, and discounts. Evaluate your scheduled activities to see if they fit your itinerary.

Can I use a credit card in Amsterdam?

Credit cards are generally accepted. However, it is advisable to have sufficient cash, particularly for smaller shops or markets.

How is the public transportation system in Amsterdam?

Amsterdam's public transit system is efficient and includes trams, buses, and metros. The city is also bike-friendly, and you can simply rent a bicycle for a true Dutch experience.

Are there any family-friendly activities in Amsterdam?

Absolutely! Family-friendly attractions include the NEMO Science Museum, the ARTIS Amsterdam Royal Zoo, and Vondelpark. Many museums have interactive exhibitions for youngsters.

At what age is it permissible to buy and consume alcohol or attend coffee shops?

The legal age to buy and use alcohol is 18. Individuals above the age of 18 are permitted to enter coffee shops where cannabis is sold.

How can I tour Amsterdam's canals?

You can discover the canals by taking a canal cruise, renting a private boat, or visiting a canal-side café with a waterfront outlook.

Is it necessary to buy tickets for museums and attractions in advance?

It is highly advised, particularly for famous attractions such as the Anne Frank House, Rijksmuseum, and Van Gogh Museum, to avoid long lines and ensure your visit.

Can I speak English in Amsterdam?

Yes, most Dutch people speak great English. However, learning a few Dutch phrases is always beneficial.

How safe is Amsterdam for tourists?

Amsterdam is generally safe for visitors. Take standard safety precautions, such as being mindful of your surroundings and belongings, and you should enjoy a trouble-free visit.

Are there any recommended day trips from Amsterdam?

Yes, popular day visits include Zaanse Schans for windmills, Keukenhof Gardens for flowers (seasonal), and Haarlem for a wonderful Dutch town atmosphere.

What is the tipping protocol in Amsterdam?

Tipping is not required but appreciated. A tip of 5-10% is usual in restaurants while service charges are typically included in the bill.

How can I try local cuisine in Amsterdam?

For a real gastronomic experience, visit local markets such as Albert Cuypmarkt, sample Dutch cheeses, eat street food, and dine at classic Dutch restaurants.

How's the weather in Amsterdam, and what should I pack?

Amsterdam has a marine climate. Pack layers, a waterproof jacket, and suitable walking shoes, and tailor your wardrobe to the season of your vacation.

Explore AMSTERDAM | 223

Scan The Code Below to Download Your Bonus

(Explore HONDURAS 2024)

About The Author

Ethan Foster is a passionate explorer, storyteller, and wanderer. With an insatiable thirst for adventure, I've committed my life to solving the world's mysteries and sharing my findings with fellow travelers.

Ethan's words, photos, and captivating lectures bring the globe closer to individuals who yearn for adventure. His publications are both a source of enjoyment and a great resource for fellow travelers, providing practical advice and insights for those wishing to follow in his footsteps.

Gain Access to More Books from Me

Printed in Great Britain
by Amazon